After the Casseroles

REDISCOVERING HOPE IN GRIEF'S JOURNEY

After the Casseroles
REDISCOVERING HOPE IN GRIEF'S JOURNEY

J.T. JONES

REDEMPTION
PRESS

Published by Redemption Press, PO Box 427, Enumclaw, WA 98022. Toll Free (844) 2REDEEM (273-3336)

Redemption Press is honored to present this title in partnership with the author. The views expressed or implied in this work are those of the author. Redemption Press provides our imprint seal representing design excellence, creative content and high quality production.

New Revised Standard Version Bible, copyright 1989, Division of Christian Education of the National Council of the Churches of Christ in the United States of America. Used by permission. All rights reserved.

No other versions used.

ISBN 13: 978-1-68314-096-2
Library of Congress Catalog Card Number: 2016950246

Dedication

IT IS WITH my deepest sense of appreciation I dedicate this book to all those who have shared their grief journey with me in more than twenty years of my facilitating bereavement support groups. These brave and wounded souls are my true teachers and my mentors.

Also to Jessie Mae Jones, my paternal grandmother. It was through her diaries I learned that the day comes when there are no more casseroles for every bereaved soul.

And to my late brother, Bruce Alan Jones, MD. Bruce was a driving force in bringing Hospice care to Lenawee County, Michigan. At the time of his death in 1990, he was the medical Director of Hospice of Lenawee. Scores of families have been helped because of Bruce's foresight in palliative care, his uncompromising compassion, and his dedication to those whom he served.

Contents

Special Thanks

THERE IS NO conceivable way this material could have moved from concept to reality without the help of many others.

To Michael Hurst and Andrew Hurst, who generously offered their support, a venue for caring, and their unreserved encouragement, I am deeply appreciative.

To the compassionate Hospice bereavement support group facilitators, LuAnn Arnson and Annemarie Anderson, from whom I learned so much about bereavement and simply how to care for others in life's toughest journey.

To Patrice Fulton-Peacock, parish nurse, who taught me the gentle skill of listening and affirming.

To Larry Moss for his keen insights as a wordsmith and advisor; I am most grateful.

To Linda Newton for her advice and valued insights.

To Susan Alderden, whose affirming voice in support of this project spoke from the depth of her own grief journey. Susan's comments were helpful as one who truly understood what it means when there are no more casseroles.

To the many who have shared their grief journeys with me in bereavement support groups over more than two decades. In having openly shared their stories, these many dozens of people, searching for hope and healing, gave me an immeasurable library of insight into bereavement. I have used some of their stories but have fiercely protected their confidentiality. We can learn much from their grief journeys. All names are changed and every identity will be protected for eternity.

I particularly thank my grandmother, Jessie M. Jones, for driving out of her way every Sunday morning to take me to church when I was a child. That simple kindness ultimately led me to become a Christian pastor. It was my widowed Gran Jessie who also wrote in her diary

". . . it has been a long time since anyone has sent a casserole." Those dozen words gave birth to both this book and to helping others in their grief journey.

In Christ,
J. T. Jones

Preface

—⚭—

MY PATERNAL GRANDFATHER died at age forty as the result of a farming accident. My grandmother remained a widow until her death at age ninety-two. She was never able to fully recover her emotional, spiritual, and mental equilibrium in her six decades of widowhood. She lived a long life that was filled with all manner of busyness. She seemed to function as a distant observer to her family and her community. In many ways, hers was a sad existence that was often punctuated with bouts of depression. She called those her "glum days."

My grandmother was a lifelong diary keeper. From her teen years until the dark veil of dementia descended on her late years, she logged the events of every day of her life. After her death, I read many of her journals. I was particularly interested in the events that followed an October afternoon in 1944, the day my grandfather was attacked and gored by a bull. He died only hours after that gruesome mauling.

Her diary recorded the event in great detail. She told of neighbors who came with condolences and casseroles. She wrote about the memorial service. She chronicled the cost of the funeral. Over the following weeks, she wrote of the visitors, the cards, the calls, and the outreach of many who were touched by my grandfather's death.

She told of the dozens of neighbors who came to the farm one Saturday morning, and before the sun set that day, all the crops were harvested. A farm work bee was common in those days and spoke to a deep sense of belonging within the community. When one suffered, all suffered. They were practical folk who never overlooked the most basic of human needs when crisis struck a member of the community. She was the recipient of a remarkable outpouring of compassion by a caring community in the form of calls, cards, and casseroles. Their practicality did not ignore who would milk the cows, gather the eggs, fill the granary, and till the land.

There was a single entry in her diary about six months after his death. In her cramped writing style with its distinctive slant, she wrote:

> I am so sad. I am so blue. No one calls. No one comes. No one even mentions my beloved Henry's name. It has been a long time since anyone has sent a casserole. They must have all forgotten.

Those fewer than forty words pierced my heart. In her glum moment that was awash in melancholy, she had brilliantly stated one of the central truths regarding grief. People care, but eventually they move on. It was clear she had come face-to-face with this solemn reality. The bereaved linger in their sorrow, while the well-meaning and deeply-caring go on about their lives. It is a natural human response for those who grieve to feel forgotten. It is not a critique on how much or how little we care. Rather, it is simply human nature. Those closest to the death of a loved one often feel abandoned in our eventual absence. Loneliness sets in, and too often if unaddressed, it tends to stay.

No more casseroles was more than a metaphor for my grandmother. It was how she measured her perceived abandonment. There had been hundreds who showed their respects, shed tears with her, reached deeply into their lives and offered support in many ways. But now they had all gone home and back to their busy lives. Simply put, there were no more calls, no more cards, and no more casseroles.

The journey though grief nearly always comes down to an individual trudge. It is not that family, friends, neighbors, or faith communities no longer care. It is more a matter of practicality. Those closest to the death are far more deeply affected than those who care from a distance. For the bereaved, the result is the feeling of abandonment. The bereaved may feel abandoned by family, friends, neighbors, faith community, and even by God. The aloneness that comes with the passing of a loved one is seldom one of fleeting sorrow. Grief seeps into every facet of the bereaved's life. It brings disarray in one's physical, mental, emotional, financial, and spiritual well-being. Tragically, this great malaise is too often endured alone.

There comes a time after every death when everyone goes home. For a moment, the brief respite from the crowd of caring folk may be welcome. As a friend once said, "When my mother died, so many people wanted to hug me that I just got my fill of hugs." A time to grieve alone, to weep openly, and even to boldly and loudly scream one's deep sense of frustration may feel liberating. However, one soon learns that the loneliness is exacerbated by aloneness. If there ever were a time when we need people, it is in the grief journey.

As a tribute to my grandmother and the millions of others who endure unresolved grief, I humbly offer these strategies on how to rediscover purpose, meaning, and the resolve that will lead to a healing heart. These are practical ideas that are soundly based in a faith in God's grace, but are not the exclusive domain of any particular religion. The following pages are filled with the healing experience I have gleaned from working with hundreds of bereaved persons. These strategies will help the bereaved better understand the grief journey. The common pitfalls found along the road to healing will be clearly explored. Many proven and practical ideas will be offered on how to deal with loneliness, celebrate holidays, regain strength, and rediscover hope when faced with life's harshest sorrow.

Most of all, my greatest hope for the bereaved is to learn how to dine on hope when there are no more casseroles.

Purpose

THE HOPE FOR those who read this book is to receive assistance on the uncharted journey through grief following the death of a loved one. Regardless the cause of death, the reader's relationship to the deceased, or how recent or long ago the death occurred, the central goals remain the same. They are:

- To provide a sense of belonging and help bereaved individuals to begin to understand the scope of grief

- To help recently bereaved persons learn the skills of how to live alongside the grief that accompanies the death of a loved one

- To address and validate the spiritual, emotional, and physical brokenness that often accompanies grief

- To reconnect bereaved persons with a life of worth and purposeful living

- To develop within bereaved persons a source of help and encouragement for future persons in the midst of the grieving process

Bereavement Myths and Facts

— ❦ —

Myth: Immersing myself in busyness will cure my grief.
Fact: A busy mind does offer temporary escape from grief, but unfortunately it is only a short-lived fix.

Myth: I am a strong person. I can deal with my sorrow on my own.
Fact: Perhaps you can rediscover a sense of bliss on your own, but that has little to do with strength.

Myth: Support groups are for weak people.
Fact: Support groups are for all bereaved people.

Myth: Fewer tears are proof that I am getting past my grief.
Fact: Tears are not a standard of measurement on the scale of bereavement.

Myth: If I have a difficult time with sorrow it means I am not a person of faith.

Fact: The death of a loved one brings deep sorrow to believers and nonbelievers alike. Faith is an important tool for many in the healing journey, but it was never intended to fully protect one in the time of loss.

Myth: Grieving the death of a loved one should last about a year.

Fact: There is no right or wrong time frame for grieving. How long it takes can differ from person to person.

Myth: Simple faith-based solutions will quickly bring about healing.

Fact: Clichés don't cut it! "He/she is in a better place." True, but I want him/her here with me.

Myth: The best plan for a speedy recovery is to ignore my grief.

Fact: Trying to ignore your pain or keep it from surfacing will only make it worse. For real healing, it is necessary to face your grief and actively deal with it. To ignore grief is like putting it in a mason jar and placing the jar on the top shelf of the pantry. One day it will ferment and explode. Likely that explosion will happen when least expected and at the most inopportune time. Grief must be addressed, even if doing so brings initial discomfort.

PART I

THE GRIEF JOURNEY

Chapter 1

What Is this Thing Called Bereavement?

TO BE BEREAVED is to be plunged into a state of unrelenting grief and sorrow. Bereavement is the shared state of sorrow following the death of a loved one. To be bereaved is to be deeply saddened by death.

There is a commonality to bereavement. It has rather predictable stages. Psychiatrist Dr. Elizabeth Kubler-Ross was a pioneer in studying the subject of dying. Her work, *On Death and Dying*, published in 1969, was a groundbreaking study on a long-neglected subject. Kubler-Ross presented five stages of death most terminally ill patients have in common. They are: denial, anger, bargaining, depression, and acceptance. In her last published book, which is lesser known, she wrote on grief with the same keen mind for observation. In *On Grief and Grieving*, she studied the syndrome of bereavement.

Both of these works are classics in their respective fields and each helped to shape and inform much of what we know today about end-of-life issues and the healing journey for the survivors. Before Kubler-Ross, dying and bereavement were not well-studied topics. We, the living, owe her a deep sense of gratitude for the work she did to start the conversation we now have in this most important part of life.

It has been argued that no culture has ever been capable of fully embracing both ends of the spectrum of life. The Victorians, who endured gruesome wars and high infant mortality, had much to say about death. Victorian literature and art focus on death, but at the expense of human sexuality. The same can be said for our ancestors from the Puritan tradition. In our time, the pendulum has swung to the opposite end. Our movies, literature, and art are filled with sex, while avoiding even considering death as much as possible. It is no great surprise that those who are bereaved feel like they are going against the grain of our modern world.

Like Kubler-Ross' theory of predictable stages of dying, there is a large pool of symptoms that often accompany bereavement. One might have several or many of these common symptoms, which range from poor appetite, sleeplessness, inability to control emotions to confusion, listlessness, fatigue, rage, depression, and a myriad of other possibilities. These form a somewhat predictable routine we refer to as the bereavement syndrome.

The sorrow one endures following a loved one's death is part of the human condition.

We are one in bereavement. It is common to being human. The sorrow one endures following a loved one's death is part of the human condition. The only way to avoid ever having to deal with grief is to never love another. However, to live a loveless life would be exponentially worse than to suffer grief.

The particular events leading up to your loved one's death, or the cause of death, can add additional layers to your grief. Suicide, AIDS, Sudden Infant Death Syndrome (SIDS), murder, medical malpractice, alcoholism, or drug abuse can bring along additional layers of guilt, anger, or a feeling of powerlessness.

However, death is death. Regardless of the cause of your loved one's passing from this life, every bereaved person holds in common a deep sense of loss. Additionally, there is often some measure of anger and feelings of powerlessness and confusion.

To compare stories is a futile endeavor. A long, lingering illness does allow for some degree of acceptance over the shock of a sudden and unexpected death. Yet one cannot pre-grieve. No matter how difficult and lingering the final chapter might be, we are still caught in the grip of sorrow. The reality is never fully grasped until your loved one passes from this life.

Think of your present state of grief as one of cause and response. Cause matters little; your response matters a lot.

Chapter 2

Moving on When You Feel Stuck

⟿⟁◌

TRAGICALLY FOR THE bereaved, the cards, the calls, and the casseroles cease. The ever-present well-wishers who repeatedly promised, "If there is anything I can do," have gone about their own busy lives.

Grief is like a pebble dropped in a pool. The inner circles of ripples are the deepest and the most impacted. The outer circles are but vanishing ripples that soon become tranquil waters. Those closest to the deceased feel the most impact and are the ones who feel the most abandoned by their family, friends, and community. From deep within the bereaved comes the lament of abandonment: "Have they all forgotten?"

> *From deep within the bereaved comes the lament of abandonment: "Have they all forgotten?"*

The feeling of abandonment, coupled with one's questioning his or her mental status, are markers of the inadequacy of the resources to bring about healing. The feeling that you are alone and ill

5

prepared to move on is a familiar cry from the bereaved. This imbalance of resources and needs prolongs the grief process.

One solution to this feeling of abandonment and the overwhelming feeling of inadequacy is to seek outside help. An inherent part of being human is to recognize that in every life there are those times when you simply do not have the necessary resources to meet life's challenges.

An archeologist came upon an ancient thigh bone that showed the marks of having been broken and then later healed. The archeologist concluded that this healed thigh bone may have been one of the first signs of caring for another. In a hunting and gathering culture, one who could neither hunt nor gather soon starved. Someone cared for, nurtured, and loved that lame soul back to life. The same is true for the bereaved. We, too, need the care and nurture of others if we are to heal.

In our feeling of abandonment and aloneness, we begin to feel like the old cartoon character, Popeye. When pressed to his limit, Popeye would say, "That's all I can stands, I can't stands no more!"

We need each other. We need another most in time of crisis. Popeye's solution was to eat a can of spinach. The bereaved's solution is to seek outside help.

There is no single source of help that holds a monopoly on healing a broken heart. A visit to your primary care physician is a good starting place to seek outside help. A family member or a friend can fill that void of abandonment. A faith community or a clergy member can help with assurance and affirmation. A skilled counselor can help move the bereaved from brokenness to healing. Hospice, Compassionate Friends, and other support groups can be enormously helpful in designing strategies that lead toward healing.

Having personally observed many participants working together with a skilled facilitator in a bereavement support group, I can say that these groups are hugely helpful. They are the most affordable, most practical, and most universally helpful resource to anyone who is grieving the death of a loved one. Bereavement support groups are available in nearly every community in our country. They vary some in scope and curricula offered. However, these groups all share in common a safe and confidential place to spill out your deepest hurts and concerns. A support group does not smother one with platitudes, scripture, or clichés. A quality support group addresses the grief journey without judgment. They offer no quick fixes, but rather help to teach the skills of how to live alongside one's grief on a daily basis.

Be sure to understand it takes a measure of courage to become part of a bereavement support group. Allowing others to hear your pain and inviting strangers to see your sorrow are never easy. You, and your emotions, are vulnerable in the presence of others. These groups can be a challenge for the timid. However, when you are beaten down, left resourceless, and feel abandoned, where else can you turn?

Think of attending a bereavement support group in the same way you would consider signing up at a fitness center. The first few trips to the gym are painful. Over time, as you work those neglected muscles, you become stronger and the pain subsides. In a bereavement support group, you are working your heart muscle. At first, your heart will rebel with pain. As time goes on, you will become stronger.

Chapter 3

How Will I Know When to Seek Help?

~)))©

WHEN WILL I know? There is no definitive answer to that question. If you have considered harming yourself or another, the answer is a resounding *immediately!* Such destructive thoughts demand instant action. Self-destructive behaviors have an insidious way of courting your better senses. What seemed unthinkable at another time in your life may now loom as reasonable possibilities. Seek immediate help if you are contemplating harming yourself or another.

For all others, the answer is a seemingly ambiguous *sooner* or *later*. One woman attended a bereavement support group only a few days after her husband's death in an auto accident.

Another sought help eleven years after cancer took her spouse of forty-eight years.

Generally, during a window of two to six months following the death of a loved one is a good time to seek help. Remember, in the early weeks in the life of the bereaved there are still calls, cards, and casseroles. When the aloneness begins to settle in, and you begin to question your sanity, that is a good time to start thinking about finding a support group.

Two to six months following a loved one's death, the feeling of abandonment is common. The casseroles come no more. This is the time to take the initiative to seek help. If you choose to delay your asking for help until a later date, that is fully acceptable. It is really a matter of individual choice.

An old adage reminds us that time heals everything. There may be a nugget of truth in that. No one can deny that over time the sharp edge of memory dulls a bit. Yet the passage of time is not the friend of the bereaved seeking to rediscover hope. Time dulls the memory as the grieving heart awaits hope. The matter of grief demands action. It requires an honest inventory of oneself. It is going to take courage and strength to overcome this unwelcome guest that has taken up residence in your life. It will take time, but time in and of itself is not the sole prescription for healing and hope. I caution you to not rely exclusively on time as a cure for your grief.

Psalm 46:1 God is our refuge and strength, a very present help in trouble.

Chapter 4

Getting Started

~⊗~

To the Bereaved, the Cruelest Word is Still.

"HOW ARE YOU doing, Carol?"

"Oh, I have my good days and my bad days. I guess I'm doing as well as can be expected. It has been almost a year, and I miss him every day."

"Still?"

The one syllable question is a cutting indictment of the bereaved in a variety of ways. It asks, "Where is your faith? Where is your strength? Why haven't you moved on? Why so long?"

The word *still* is a clear reminder that your ongoing sorrow is overlooked, trivialized, and surely misunderstood by a well-meaning friend. It sets up a standard of how long a normal (whatever normal might be) grieving period should last. "Still" says, in that person's view, you have gone far beyond the norm. It is also a blatant reminder that the world has moved on, while you remain mired in grief. That simple one-word question is about as cruel as life can get for the bereaved.

There is no absolute standard for how long the bereaved will struggle with deep, encompassing, and unrelenting sorrow. There is no definitive date when the dark veil of a broken heart will once again know joy. There are many factors that will determine how deep one descends into sorrow and how long the bereaved will remain in the realm of grief. Gender, past experience, culture, age, relationship to the deceased, economic situation, and a myriad of other factors play a role in one's journey to wholeness. The "still" of it all varies widely and is particular to each individual.

> *There is no absolute standard for how long the bereaved will struggle with deep, encompassing, and unrelenting sorrow.*

The Victorian tradition was to wear black clothes or a black arm band for one year. This was a signal to the world that you were in mourning. It was a silent cultural warning that gaiety was to be avoided. The mourning garb was also a visible reminder that you were not a candidate for courtship. Off came the long black veil or arm band on the first anniversary of a loved one's death. The new wardrobe was a symbol of normalcy having returned. It was now visible to all that the mourning time had come to a close. Often the pain of sorrow still lingered within, but the world only saw that symbol of normalcy that proclaimed healing.

If only it were as simple as looking at the calendar and changing your clothes. Healing the wounds that follow the death of a loved one is far from that simple. For some, the second year is tougher than the first year. For others, a wondrous healing and a new sense of resolve have unfolded. For many, seeking help from a grief counselor, hospice, a religious community, clergy, or family member or friend can be enormously helpful. There is no life that has all the necessary resources to meet every one of life's challenges. Seeking support is not a weakness, nor is it an admission of failure. Turning to a family member, a friend, or a professional while in the clutch of grief is no different than going to a physician when one is ill. The good news for the bereaved is that there are numerous resources that can help on the road to healing.

In the following chapters we will explore a variety of topics that all point to one common goal: how to live alongside your grief. It is not intended to be a road map to total happiness, but rather an introduction to the skills that lead to a life once again filled with hope, meaning, and reasonable contentment. Though faith is a vital part of recovery, in this section we will focus more on the practical aspects of rediscovering a sense of bliss, rather than the torment of sorrow.

The following chapters will open new possibilities that the reader may not have considered. This material will also focus on validating the deep and mysterious anguish that accompanies the death of a loved one. For many of us, bereavement is an uncharted path that can make us question our sanity. We need to be heard, affirmed, and comforted. We need compassionate listeners rather than zealous fixers. We need one another.

So let's get started . . .

Chapter 5

Taking a Grief Inventory

—◦❦◦—

WE OFTEN ARE asked, "How are you doing?" The most common answer is, "About as well as can be expected."

Tragically, the question is not always sincere. It may not be any more than trying to begin a conversation by talking about the weather. Mark Twain once said, "If the weather never changed, most people couldn't begin a conversation."

For the grieving one: *What am I supposed to say? How am I supposed to feel? What is the expectation? What's the standard of sorrow? Do you really want to know how miserable I feel?* It is just easier to turn to the ambiguous answer that reveals little: "About as well as can be expected."

Doug Manning is a prolific author on the subject of grief counseling. Manning expresses his belief in the importance of taking a Grief Inventory. Such an inventory will help the bereaved to have a better and well-thought-out answer when asked, "How are you doing?" Moreover, a grief inventory will help the bereaved person have a better self-understanding of how he or she really feels.

It is important to know that you have permission to grieve. Grieving is not just okay; it is essential to the healing process.

It is important to know that you have permission to grieve.

Far too many of us want to hurry the process and get past the hurt, the tears, and the mind-numbing sorrow of a loved one's passing. It is like a severe cold. The sooner it is over, the sooner we can get on with our lives. Like the common cold, in grieving we have little control over the symptoms: the misery, the tears, or the duration of our grief. *In short, on our own we are often powerless in the face of grief.* The beginning of healing is simply accepting both the magnitude of our grief and our powerlessness to get past it.

A second consideration for denying our grief is that it tends to diminish the person for whom we grieve. "I'm doing fine," is often dishonest and trivializes the magnitude of our loss. Here is where a Grief Inventory can help. We really do not know what we have lost until we honestly face our loss. How many times have we quietly said to ourselves: "I wish I had told them." "I wish I had asked." "I hope they knew."

These are thoughts that can begin the conversation about how important that person was and is in your life. A Grief Inventory is one way of measuring the worth of your loved one in your own life.

The matter of denial is common to the bereaved. Many take a critical approach to denial. They see it as a primitive response or a childish fix. Actually, denial is an expected and healthy part of the healing process. It allows time to filter the reality of our hurt. It is not beyond reason to believe that denial is a God-given reaction to keep us from harm. Without a bit of denial, perhaps the shock of a loved one's death would simply be too much for any one of us to bear.

Think of denial as a temporary fix. Suppose you had a cherished grand piano. Somehow one of the piano's legs was broken. You were in a hurry. You did not want to deal with, or perhaps could not afford, the proper repair the dignified grand piano deserved. So you got a roll of duct tape and wrapped the piano leg with the silver sticky stuff. It served its purpose. The piano stood straight and tall. The quality of its sound was not affected. The duct tape did the trick.

However, deep down you knew this was only a temporary fix. One day you took the time to remove the duct tape, drill a few holes in the piano leg, hammer wooden pegs into the holes, liberally glue the broken leg, allow it to dry and harden, sand it all down to a silky finish, and then refinish the leg to its original beauty. It was a long process with many steps. It took time. In truth, the piano still had some evidence of its once-fractured leg, but now it was ready for center stage and Carnegie Hall.

The journey through bereavement is like the broken piano leg. Complete restoration is possible, but it takes time with many steps along the way. The finished product might still have a bit of evidence of fracture, but it is surely more beautiful than duct tape on a grand piano.

You do not have to apologize for denial. You are in good and plentiful company. However, think of denial as a temporary stage along the way to recovery, rather than a permanent and lasting fix. Taking an inventory of your grief is the first step in breaking down the barrier of denial. Though it is hard, gutsy, and painful work, it is the beginning of the healing journey. Think of it as tearing off the duct tape and getting the tools together to recreate a thing of beauty.

A Grief Inventory will often take you back to remembering touches, conversations, shared experiences, victories and defeats, tough times and successes, the beauty of shared sunsets, a newborn's smile, fears and fears overcome, lessons learned and lessons taught, and the experience of living through many of life's passages (some invited and some not so welcome). It has been said, "We are the sum total of our experience." When a loved one dies, you are left alone to tally up that sum total of both what you lost and who you are. Your Grief Inventory has one purpose: It is to honestly acknowledge how much this person meant to you.

Chapter 6

Grief Inventory

AS I CONSIDER how my life has changed from the loss of my loved one, I find an emptiness or a missing piece in a variety of places. I mostly miss:

Psalm 34:18 The Lord is near to the brokenhearted, and saves the crushed in spirit.

My best friend

My handyman/fixer of things

My helpmate

My reflection of self

One to carry on my name

My interior decorator

My painter

My keeper of secrets

My housekeeper/homemaker

My intimate partner

My stake in the future

My landscaper

My driver/chauffeur

My artistic advisor

My trip planner

My financial planner

One who made me a better person

A piece of me

My carrier of heavy things

My keeper of the family history

My encourager

My organizer

My meal partner

One who made me whole

One who wiped away my tears

My spiritual advisor

One who listened to my complaining

My promise keeper

My excuse for the parts of me I didn't like

My person who saw beauty in all things

Other:

My source of laughter

My moral compass

My encyclopedia of wisdom

One who spoiled me

His/her touch

My caregiver

My reminder of important things

My comforter

My affirmer

My entertainer

My financial supporter

My grooming advisor

My soul mate

One who overlooked my flaws

My explainer

My speller of hard words

My chief defender

Chapter 7

Setting Goals

A GRIEF INVENTORY will help identify the scope of your loss. Of course much of what that inventory reveals is far from news to you. Perhaps the enormity of your loss is better understood when you take a searching and careful inventory. It will also point out your particular areas of vulnerability. A careful, searching, and brave inventory of your loss will help you to set some preliminary goals.

These beginning goals are preliminary. They are a beginning point that will lead you to greater endeavors. Remember, you are showing up at the heart exercise gym for the first time. You will need to take your time. You will need to be patient. And you will need to be open to going beyond the initial goals. Granted, these first steps are challenging, but they are achievable. Start easy and new goals will unfold.

One man, whose wife died suddenly and unexpectedly, said his main concern was to learn how to do his own laundry. He couldn't remember which of those alike-looking machines was the washer and which was the dryer.

A woman, who was nearly paralyzed by grief, set her primary goal as hoping to one day be able to walk down the driveway and collect her mail.

The mother of a teenage boy who took his own life wanted to have the courage to be able to say the word "suicide."

Still another set the goal of being able to write a few words in his daily journal again. He had been a life-long diary keeper and he had lost the ability and the ambition to pick up a pen and write a few words.

Goals need not be elaborate. Simple is best. A goal needs to be measurable and achievable. To set a goal to feel better is hard to measure. Feeling better is difficult to quantify. To set the goal of absolute and complete happiness is not reasonable nor is it achievable. Life, even in its best of times, has its sweet moments and its bitter times.

> *Life, even in its best of times, has its sweet moments and its bitter times.*

To wish to make progress toward wholeness by overcoming fear, anxiety, and hopelessness is hard to measure. However, to work toward that end is surely a reasonable endeavor.

You might consider some of the following for your initial goals:

- Get all my thank you notes written and mailed.
- Begin to take better care of myself. i.e., get a physical, visit the hair salon, buy a new suit, change the oil in the car, or start eating a more balanced diet.
- Return to my seat in the church choir.
- Create a scrapbook of memories.
- Sort his or her closet and other personal items. I'll give to family members the items that need to stay in the family. Then I'll give the rest to some worthy charity.
- Get my checkbook balanced.
- Take a child fishing.
- File my income tax that is now six months past due.

Chapter 8

Forming a Plan

ASK ANY BEREAVEMENT counselor or clergy member and they will all agree that they have often heard a grieving person say, "I think I'm losing it."

The death of a loved one does cause one to question one's sanity. He or she is plunged into a dark realm of paralyzing sorrow, loneliness, confusion, and bewilderment. For many, it is uncharted waters. Thankfully, the death of a loved one is not a frequent

> *The death of a loved one does cause one to question one's sanity.*

happening in one's life. So we have no familiar frame of reference to rely upon. We cannot say, "Every time someone close to me dies, this is what I need to do."

It is a frightening realization to question one's sanity. A perfectly normal reaction to the death of someone close is to feel isolated and confused. We tend to have difficulty focusing on the simplest tasks. We can become forgetful. We spend a disproportionate amount of time wallowing in the "What ifs."

We may become consumed with anger. Our rage might be focused on the deceased for leaving us. We might blame the victim for poor choices that led to death, *i.e.,* smoking, eating habits, failure to seek medical help, or reckless lifestyle choices. Perhaps our blame is focused on the medical community for what we perceive as malpractice or simple incompetence. We might blame God (more will be said about blaming God in a later section). Anger is a close cousin to grief.

We may tend to seek isolation. Most of us were reared in a culture that frowns on public display of emotions. We feel embarrassed if we break down and cry in public. The natural response to shedding tears in public is to control the part of that equation we can. We are powerless to control our tears, so we simply avoid public gatherings. This isolation contributes to an even deeper sense of depression.

The bereaved may become disinterested in eating, sleeping, or self-care. Perhaps reaching out for some form of escape in drugs, alcohol, food, sex, or gambling brings a bit of respite from the daily grind of grief. Any, or all, of these abuses will only exacerbate one's grief and stand as a barrier to lasting recovery.

Another area common to the bereaved is the matter of visions, signs, dreams, sightings, and mystical experiences. These often seem so real and yet remain inexplicable.

Louise's mother died after a long illness. Louise was a devout Christian but was deeply troubled about her mother's salvation. The matter of the destiny of her mother's soul unrelentingly tormented her. If only she had some way of knowing. In a dream, Louise saw her mother ascending a long stairway. When her mother reached the top of the stairs, just before she became invisible in the clouds, she stopped, looked at Louise, and waved goodbye. Louise saw this as proof her mother had entered heaven. She was now at peace because she now believed her mother was at peace.

Another woman tells of awakening in the night from a deep sleep. She felt the presence of her deceased husband in the darkened bedroom. She rolled over and felt a hollow spot in the mattress and that depression in the bedding felt warm.

Darlene and Jeff's son died unexpectedly at age thirty. He was the family's grill master. Whenever they gathered for a family cookout, their son was in charge of the grilling. It was his passion and joy. One sunny afternoon Darlene and Jeff sat in the screened-in porch looking out at the backyard while enjoying a cool lemonade. Suddenly, a single branch on the large oak tree that shaded the grill began to shimmy and shake. It was a perfectly still day with not a wisp of breeze. No other plant, shrub, or tree was moving. At first they thought a squirrel or a bird was shaking the oak branches. Jeff went out and inspected the strange quaking in the tree. There was no squirrel, no bird, and no obvious reason the branches over the grill appeared to be whipping in the wind on a windless day. Jeff was able to video the event as proof they were not imagining this unexplainable event. Both Darlene and Jeff saw this as a sign that their son was back in his favorite place at the grill.

Over more than two decades of counseling hundreds of bereaved persons, I have heard these stories of dreams, sightings, signs, and visions far too many times to believe they are merely the imagination of an individual under stress. I have come to believe there is a mysterious realm of consciousness that invites many bereaved persons into a deeper understanding. None of these unexplainable events were expected or planned, nor is it to be understood that everyone will be affirmed with one of these dreams or visions. They occur often, but not always, and surely cannot be planned, conjured up, or arranged. To say they are real, yet they remain a mystery, is sufficient.

For most, these visions are a comforting reassurance that their loved one is safe and, at some level, present to them. For

some, these sightings, signs, dreams, and visions compound their
bewilderment and cause them to even further ask: Am I losing it?

If there is anything to be gleaned from a Grief Inventory,
it is the solid and tangible evidence that a loved one's death has
taken a huge toll in your life. It confronts you on many levels.
Thus it is surely reasonable to wonder about your sanity. Are
you losing it? In nearly every case the answerer is: "*No!*" You
are suffering from grief. It wears many masks and is constantly
making its presence known in every aspect of life. Grief is not
like a stone in your shoe that causes a minor irritation. It is more
like a large nail protruding through the soles of both shoes. Every
step you take is confronted with unrelenting pain.

A Grief Inventory is a sound beginning point. However,
merely acknowledging the scope of the loss does little to welcome
healing. Rather, coming to grips with the reality of one's loss
does help to develop a plan of action. The first step in forming
a plan for recovery is validation. You are not yourself, simply
because you are deeply wounded by grief. Be assured that all the
unmanageability in your life—from anger to confusion, from
depression to disinterest, and from sleeplessness to shaking your
angry fist at God—has nothing to do with your loss of sanity.
You are grieving, and that is more than enough to cause you to
ask, "Am I losing it?"

Second, know that healing is possible and achievable.

Fred's spouse died after a lengthy battle with cancer. He had
been a loving and dutiful caregiver to her. Naturally, Fred felt a
huge emptiness after his wife of more than forty years died. He
slipped into a deep funk and major depression. He filled his days
by reading mystery novels. Fred readily admitted that he had no
idea what was the plot or the outcome of any of the novels. He
was so lost in grief that the five to seven books a week he read
were no more than chewing gum from his despair.

Fred made an appointment with a pastoral counselor. He
quietly admitted that he saw no good reason to go on living. Yet

Fred did not want to die. He was not actively considering suicide, but he had grown weary of his present life of nothingness. He felt his purpose, his meaning, and his worth had been plucked from his soul. He explained that money was no problem: He owned a beautiful home and had all the luxuries to go with it. He had reasonably good health; Fred's two daughters did all they could to try to cheer him; his grandchildren gave him a bit of joy; but without his soul mate, life just didn't seem worth living. He asked those familiar questions: "Am I losing it and will I ever get better?"

Fortunately for Fred, the pastoral counselor had heard those questions many times in the past. The counselor's answer was an affirming, "No, you are not losing it, and yes, you will get better."

Fred was silent for a full minute and then asked, "Do you really think so?"

"Unquestionably! You are caught in grief and I assure you, there is hope for you."

Again Fred sat silently considering the counselor's words of affirmation and assurance. Then a big smile came over his face and he said, "I think you really believe that."

Fred had been affirmed and validated. He was not losing it. Rather he was suffering from unresolved grief that was not a permanent indictment on his future hope for a life of meaning. Over the next few weeks Fred and the counselor met on several occasions. In a short time, Fred began to find a new sense of bliss. It all began with the affirmation and validation that grief and insanity are not synonymous.

Chapter 9

Grief Strategies

~❦~

No Right or Wrong Way to Grieve

UNLESS WE INTEND to harm ourselves, another, or another's property, there is really no right or wrong way to grieve. Some bury themselves in busyness. Others seek spiritual or religious help. Others might find comfort in denial or seeking joy to outpace their sorrow. Some are silent. Some are vocal. Some prefer to be alone while others seek solace in crowds.

One of the least helpful bits of advice is our telling another how he or she needs to grieve. None of us needs a "Fixer." So when someone begins a conversation with, "What you need to do . . ." it is best to simply and politely say, "I'll think about that." It is good for all of us to remember we can *fix* a leaky roof, but we can never *fix* people. The kindest and most supportive action we can extend to another is simply to be a good listener and offer a compassionate heart.

The Bad News and the Good News

The bad news is that when we come face to face with grief, it tends to tear off the scabs of previous hurts. These hurts are not limited to earlier deaths we have experienced. They are about life's losses, which may include loss of youth, loss of a relationship, loss of health, loss of hope, loss of a dream, loss of a job, or any other kind of loss that caused us great duress. Tragically, we tend to relive and regrieve past sorrows. It seems a heavy load when heaped upon our current sorrow.

The *good news* is that each of us probably has far more resources than we might be aware of having. We subconsciously tend to use those tested and successful strategies of the past. If busyness helped then, we will likely immerse ourselves in busyness. If our faith pulled us through earlier hurts, we will seek religious support. Whatever seemed to bring relief in the past will most likely be the place we turn to find our current hope.

Until we come face-to-face with grief, we seldom consider our rich pool of learned life strategies. When we encounter mourning, it is only natural to revert to proven pathways to healing we have used in times of previous sorrow.

Grieving Is Hard Work

Grieving is hard and exhausting work. It encroaches on every facet of our lives. Grief can, and often does, upset us physically,

> **Grieving is hard and exhausting work.**

mentally, emotionally, spiritually, and financially. To pretend we saw this coming and we pre-grieved our loss is neither honest nor realistic. We cannot pre-grieve. It is an uninvited passage that must be addressed. Be sure to understand that many times our effort to resume some normalcy in life might seem to exacerbate our grief. We have all heard someone say, "Well, if I just ignore my loss, it hopefully will go away." To ignore seldom brings lasting healing.

Working though grief can be tedious, hard, and painful work. Remember, it is like a beginner joining an exercise program. The first few days on the treadmill makes your muscles ache. Working though grief is working your heart muscle. Your heart most likely will ache for a time, but the end result will be healing, hope, and a new outlook on life.

Chapter 10

What If?

~∞∞©

IT IS NOT uncommon for the bereaved to be plagued with a case of "What ifs?"

> What if we had done more?
> What if I had insisted on more treatments?
> What if he had taken a different way home from work?
> What if she had trusted a different physician?
> What if he had only listened to our warnings?
> What if she had married someone else?

The list of "What ifs?" is endless. Close cousins to the "What ifs" are "If I had only" or "I should have." These and others help to keep the fires of blame well-tended. These are a common, yet useless endeavor. We simply cannot go back and get a redo. Self-blame only yields a harvest of deepening sorrow. The "What ifs" are tragically incapable of changing the ultimate outcome. At best, they are no more than a fruitless exercise. At worst, they delay healing and can deepen grief.

We are mortal beings. It has been said, when we sign on for life we seldom read the fine print at the bottom of the page that explains the mortality clause. We like to think we are in control. When it comes to our mortality, or that of a loved one, we are not in control. We are not the pilots of the ship of mortality. Death is a poignant reminder of our frailty and our inability to be in total control. Thus our agonizing over what we could have done differently is a futile and destructive exercise.

Heaping blame on oneself or another exacerbates sorrow. It also stunts our growth in recovery. As long as we are blaming, searching for a cause, or assigning fault, we are grooming a sense of guilt. That guilt may be directed at ourselves, or it might be searching for a candidate to blame. In either case, the energy is wasted on the unchanging reality that our loved one is no longer with us.

The matter of pursuing the "What ifs?" can affect us in ways other than prolonged grief and delayed recovery. It can turn the blamer into a cynical, bitter, and even contemptuous individual. Blame feeds anger and hatred and grows a malignancy on our souls.

The "What ifs?" can focus blame on the loved one we mourn. We feel miserable and the cause is our loved one's refusal to follow the medical community's advice. Maybe he or she continued to smoke or to ignore a healthy lifestyle. Perhaps the one we mourn insisted on living a risky lifestyle, took unnecessary chances, or toyed with excess in dangerous ways that led to death. It is understandable to focus our blame on the recklessness that invited death. Still, blaming is a futile effort that will never change the reality of our sorrow. Moreover, while we are stuck in the negativity of blaming, we are avoiding the productive work of recovery.

Exploring what might have been done differently is probably a natural response to death. But making blame one's vocation is self-destructive and is wasted energy that could be used in a far more productive manner.

Toying with "What if?" is a natural response to a loved one's death. However, when one is stuck in the realm of the unanswerable, it is vital to take steps toward reality. First, take ownership of your powerlessness. It is far more likely that you did all you could do. Give yourself credit for all you did to encourage, care for, support, comfort, and continue to love the dying person.

Second, acknowledge the uselessness of worry. Worry cures nothing. It distracts us from the deeper issues at hand. Worry about what others might think or whom we blame is fruitless labor. Scripture reminds us of our powerlessness and the futility of worry. Jesus asks, "Can any of you by worrying add a single hour to your span of life?" (Luke 12:25).

Third, seek to come to peace with yourself. Yes, you might have lost your patience at times. Yes, there may have been times when pure exhaustion sapped your ability to do what needed to be done. Yes, it is possible that not every decision led to a perfect outcome. Yes, you are only human. Come to a sense of peace that a greater plan usurped your best efforts. Blaming oneself or others yields only futility.

Fourth, search for acceptance. There are times when our expectation and our hopes are a mismatch with reality. We can say we completely abandon ourselves to God's grand plan, but in truth we want our loved one here beside us. Accepting the reality of death, as painful as it is, cannot be easy. However, coming to a time of acceptance of this uncomfortable mismatch is one of the first steps toward healing. Cultivating a mindset of blame, worry, questioning the "why" of it all, and guilt only feeds the furnace of lingering sorrow and tends to prolong acceptance. With acceptance comes the beginning of healing.

> *With acceptance comes the beginning of healing.*

Chapter 11

Ten Ideas for Dealing with Loneliness

THE RECENTLY WIDOWED woman said, "My life feels like someone took a huge vacuum cleaner and sucked out my soul. I wander aimlessly from room to room in a vague funk. What used to take minutes to accomplish, now takes hours or days. Nights are the worst. I wonder if I will ever rediscover a life worth living?"

Loneliness is a serious matter. This widow's feelings represent a classic case of chronic loneliness. More than any of the many symptoms that accompany a grieving person is loneliness. It can be said: To a bereaved person, loneliness is public enemy #1. It tends to overwhelm one's very being. Chronic loneliness is all-encompassing and can affect how one eats, sleeps, and attends to even the most mundane chores. It is a lethargy of the physical, emotional, and spiritual self.

Some degree of loneliness is unavoidable for most bereaved persons. However, there are some practical steps one can take to overcome this troubling malaise. These may not bring instant relief. But these suggestions can, over time, soften the symptoms of loneliness and open the doors to hope and recovery.

Believe that This, Too, Shall Pass

A dear friend of mine says her favorite Bible verse is, "and it came to pass." She goes on to say, "I'm sure glad it didn't come to stay."

Think of life as a huge bookshelf. On one end is a bookend that is made up of sorrow, sickness, defeat, and loss. On the other end is a similar bookend made up of joy, victory, good health, and hope. The good news is we live out the vast majority of our lives in the great in between. We neither are destined to languish in the realm of brokenness, nor are we only to exist in the lavish empire of plenty. That great in between is a familiar place of comfort we have come to know but find elusive in our time of grief. Rediscovering the great in between is the healing we seek. Simply knowing in your mind, and believing in your heart, that you will overcome loneliness is a huge step toward reconnecting with life's great in between.

Loneliness is real and debilitating, but it is not permanent.

Loneliness is real and debilitating, but it is not permanent. This, too, shall pass. There are steps you can take that will both soften its presence and hasten its passing.

Avoid Easy or Temporary Fixes

It makes sense that any depressant can exacerbate deeper depression. Loneliness is a symptom of depression. Adding a chemical depressant to loneliness is like tossing gasoline on a fire. True, chemical depressants can bring a temporary escape from one's despair, but they always lead to deeper despondency. The social atmosphere that usually surrounds drinking environments also offers a setting for escapism, but it too is fleeting and of unlasting reward. The downside of alcohol consumption, even in modest amounts, far outweighs any lasting benefit. The same can be said for gambling establishments.

Another easy and temporary fix is entering into a new romantic relationship. Sexual intimacy can bring a dash of excitement and joy. However, one needs to sort out the complex layers of confused emotions before committing to a new relationship. Sexual intimacy only adds to the confusion and rarely has a good long-range outcome. In short, identify and avoid destructive behaviors and easy fixes. Remember, you are vulnerable in this time of grief and need to be extra cautious about your life choices.

Seek the Company of Friends

I once heard a young woman whose teenage sister had died say, "You will always remember the ones who helped you and you will never forget those who ignored you."

Reach out to friends or family members who can support and encourage you. Cherish them as you would a precious gem. A true friend is a priceless gift. There will be those whom you might expect would be a huge resource to you who seem to be absent, ineffective, or even distant. Do not try to figure out why they are so unresponsive in your time of need. They may well have valid reasons, or they might be so deep in their own time of need that they have nothing to offer.

A true friend is one who listens and does not attempt to smother you or try to fix you. I once heard it said, "A friend is someone who knows all about you and still loves you." Someone who listens much and seldom speaks, one who wipes away your tears without judgment, one who embraces with no expectation of anything in return, and one who can be trusted with your deepest feelings is more precious than gold.

Be Bold in Seeking to Meet Your Needs

You have probably have heard the well-meaning advice of a few who will tell you to be strong. The most insensitive insult that can be made to a grieving person is to say, "Haven't you gotten over that yet?"

For some it simply takes longer than it does for others. You may need to seek professional help from a bereavement counselor. Perhaps your pastor can be of comfort. It is not unreasonable that psychiatric counseling and in some cases, medical help can assist your journey through grief.

A wise friend once said, "There are many roads that lead to Milwaukee." He was pointing out that there is no single path to recovery. Do what you must do. Be bold in asking for help. Think about the number of people who have said, "If I can help in any way, just ask." Now is the time to ask. It is not a sign of weakness or lack of faith. Rather, asking for help is the admission that in every human life, there are times when you simply do not have the resources to meet your needs. That is when a trusted friend, a professional counselor, a pastor, a priest, a rabbi or a physician can make an enormous difference in your life.

Consider Group Support

I have helped facilitate Bereavement Support Groups for more than twenty years. Over that period, I have been invited into the grief journey of hundreds of bereaved persons. I have heard about every possible circumstance of death and every type of relationship to the deceased one can experience. Though I will never fully understand the dynamics of how a support group works, I have come to believe in the power of the group.

One woman said, "I know I will get beyond this, but right now it is comforting to know I am not alone." The comfort in knowing you are not alone has been echoed hundreds of times. Support groups always bring people together who are at various stages along their healing journey. Some are newly bereaved and their emotions are raw and painful. Others may have passed through that initial period of overwhelming sorrow and have some experience in the path to healing and hope. Each can be a benefit to the other.

I think of a bereavement support group in the same way I understand gravity. I have no idea how it works, but I know I am not going to fall off the planet. Explaining it and understanding it are not necessary for one to trust it and embrace it.

Turn to God for Assurance and Hope

It is far from rare to hear someone say, "I am so mad at God." Another might ask, "Why did God do this to me?"

These responses are not new, nor are they even offensive to God. God has heard it all before. In fact, God is in the business of listening to the honest laments of our hearts. The Bible offers many incidents of either an individual or an entire community that is plunged into despair and rails out at God from a place of misery. God is no stranger to hearing our rage.

There is an often-repeated three-part theme in Scripture. It goes like this:

> God hears the voice of the broken.
> God's heart is moved.
> God responds.

When you join in a conversation with God, you can be sure God is listening. Even when you lash out in anger, worry not . . . God has heard it all before. Be prepared for God to respond.

We often hear people mention prayer and meditation as if they were one and the same. Prayer is asking, while meditation is listening. When we speak to God, God listens. When we are silent before God in a time of meditation, we are listening for the voice of God in our lives. A quiet time that steps away from our anger, seeks a quiet presence, and believes in restoration, renewal, and the rebirth of hope is strong medicine toward healing.

Often we are affirmed in the simple, yet powerful, truth that God is present in our best of times and our worst of times.

Laughter Is Good for the Soul

It was shortly after the sudden and unexpected death of a family member that I felt a deep and crushing sadness. It seemed to be an all-encompassing sorrow that wanted to consume me. Nothing I tried helped to make it go away. Joy was a lost commodity, and cheer was elusive.

My wife suggested we might go to a movie. My heart was not in the matter, but mostly to avoid a lecture on you-need-to-get-out, I reluctantly agreed. We saw an Eddie Murphy movie that was outrageously funny. I left the theater that evening feeling lifted out of my sorrow. It would be far too much to say I was healed. Rather, I had enjoyed a brief and refreshing respite from my grief. I could see the possibility that this overpowering sadness was not going to be permanent. There is something wondrously and miraculously empowering in laughter.

Though I cannot explain the reason God gave us tears, it is comforting to know that God balanced the scale of life with laughter. It is more than okay to laugh again. God hears ours sorrows, but God also delights in our laughter.

Give of Yourself

When in the midst of grief, there is a prevailing powerlessness in our ability to get out and be among others. We feel stuck. It seems life would be easier if we could just pull the covers over our head and stay in bed. We get sluggish. We tend to hide. In short, we wallow in our loneliness. These feelings of isolation are typical, yet unproductive steps on the journey toward healing.

It will not be easy, and you just might have to force yourself to do it, but giving of yourself will be of more benefit to you than it is to the receiver. You will realize an exponential return on the investment of self.

Consider volunteering at your church. Ladle out mashed potatoes and gravy at a homeless shelter. Visit a children's hospital ward. Visit a person in the county jail. Volunteer to be a helper at a preschool. Read to a child. Pound nails on a Habitat for Humanity project. Shovel the snow off your neighbor's sidewalk. The list is endless, but the reward is beyond your imagination. Nothing in life has deeper meaning than doing for another. It satisfies the soul. Selfless caring lifts the spirit. It gives your life meaning and purpose. Giving of yourself is a healing balm.

Consider Getting a Pet

You may not feel up to taking on the responsibility of caring for a goldfish, walking a dog, or enjoying the indifference of a cat. Yet for many, the unconditional love offered by a pet can be a huge comfort. Many have told me they owe their healing to their animal friend.

As with all life changes after the death of a loved one, avoid rushing into acquiring a pet. You will need to look at practical considerations of space requirements, time, financial commitment, and your future ability to meet the responsibility of caring for a pet. If it works for you, there is immeasurable potential in a pet's unconditional love.

Make a Lasting Memorial to Your Loved One

As a pastor, I have officiated at more than 600 funerals. However, when my father died I did not feel I could properly celebrate his life at his memorial service. It was a time when I felt I needed to be ministered to, rather than to be the minister. I wrote a short liturgy using what I called the Candle of Remembrance for my father's funeral. After my father's passing, I used that short Candle of Remembrance closing at scores of funerals where I officiated as pastor. The giving of a Candle of Remembrance to a family, and then seeing it prominently displayed at a grandchild's graduation reception, on the altar at a wedding, or sitting on a widow's coffee table was a poignant reminder that a simple candle could hold deep and lasting meaning to these families. Those candles were also a personal reminder to me of my father's life.

Some establish a scholarship fund in their loved one's name. For others a cemetery marker, a framed football jersey, a favorite golf club hanging over the fireplace mantel, a photo, a special deer blind, or a treasured fishing lure tucked in a sacred place in the tackle box is a memorial.

A memorial keeps the memory alive. It speaks to what mattered in our loved one's life. It can take on a life of its own and keep passing on to future generations the wonder of this one who so graced our lives. A memorial need not be an elaborate shrine. A sewing basket, a well-worn pocket knife, a mounted fish hanging on the den wall, pair of cuff links, a fountain pen, a Christmas cookie cutter, or a child's favorite doll can serve as a memorial.

An infant's pair of button shoes and a thoroughly worn-out paring knife are proudly displayed in a glass cabinet in our home. The button shoes were my grandfather's first pair of leather shoes. The paring knife saw a half century of service as my grandmother canned from her two-acre garden. Just maybe a grandchild will one day turn to me and ask, "Grandpa, whose old shoes are those?" Perhaps one will ask, "What is with the old worn-out knife?"

It will be a perfect opening for me to tell their story once more.

Chapter 12

Transitions

~❦~

What If? Or If Only . . . Or I Should Have . . .

THESE AND DOZENS more are both natural and useless exercises. Such ponderings seldom change anything. At best, they only tend to stir the pot of simmering sorrow. At worst, these thoughts assign unfounded blame or add to your guilt. Yet these are a natural part of the transition journey you are now on. Waste as little time as possible mired down in the "What ifs" of life. As difficult as it might now seem, try to focus on *what can my life become, rather than what has become of me?*

Loneliness

The earlier section on loneliness speaks to how often the insidious feeling of abandonment heaps a heavy burden on the bereaved. The most common of all feelings after the death of a loved one is loneliness. It is an aching emptiness that is with you day and night. You long just to hear that person's voice once more, or their shuffle down the hallway in the middle of the night, or their unique laughter, or even to hear that person clear his or her throat while reading the newspaper. Preparing a meal, and then eating alone, is far from old times. Loneliness is a constant reminder that you are in one of life's most difficult transitions.

As with most of life's transitions, you have choices. Sadly, some address their loneliness as the way it is going to be and choose to live the life of a recluse. Others find a bit of comfort in a pet's companionship. Many, in their time of grief, rediscover the value of friendship, the worth of community, and the strength of family. Your faith community, your clubs and organizations, your neighbors, family, and friends can help fill this emptiness. You may feel reluctant about getting back into familiar circles of old friends. There is the worry that you might publicly show your brokenness. Be assured that those who care for you will fully accept your visible sorrow. At first, you have permission to simply go through the motions. It is said if you bring the body, the mind and the spirit will naturally follow.

Many turn to deepening their faith and their daily conversation with God as a proven aid to loneliness. The basic triangular foundation of our faith is that God hears the lament of our hearts, the heart of God is moved, and God responds. God is always willing to listen to the voice of God's children through prayer.

> *God hears the lament of our hearts, the heart of God is moved, and God responds.*

A word of caution: Rushing into a new relationship to cure one's loneliness is not the answer. While living with grief, you are vulnerable. You are not fully capable of making sound decisions. As covered in an earlier chapter, sex, alcohol, drugs, gambling, or out of control spending are temporary solutions to loneliness. They might fill a void for a moment, but they never work as long-term solutions.

Searching for a New Identity

Often when a spouse dies, the survivor asks, "Who am I?" Culturally, this question tends to be true for many widowed women whose personal identity was lost in their spouse's career, friends, or associates.

For some, this can also be liberating. If the bereaved person lived in the shadow of, or was dominated by their spouse, it is an opportunity to redefine one's role in life.

Doc was a successful and busy veterinarian. His wife, Joann, was always referred to as "Doc's wife." When Doc died, Joann began to ask herself: Who am I? It took some serious and deep introspection for her to define the Doc-less Joann. In time she discovered a new sense of self, an expanded circle of friends, and new interests. A new Joann emerged from her questioning of self. She was far more than "Doc's wife." She was an integral part of a successful team, as well as a talented individual.

Who Will Take Care of Me?

I cannot count the number of men I have met who cannot cook, do laundry, or run a vacuum cleaner. It is not unusual for men to remarry soon after their spouse's death. They react out of both loneliness and perceived necessity. Conversely, there is no shortage of women who cannot back the fifth-wheel camper into a camping space. Simply because they never had the opportunity, they have never tried to balance the checkbook. Many do not know which plumber to call when the toilet runs over. Both men and women are often left not just unprepared, but tragically unprepared.

Here again is to be found the worth of family, friends, faith community, and your Creator. You have heard it said many times in life: "If I can do anything for you, just let me know." Now is the time to respond to some of those offers others have made to you. Your pastor, your friends, a support group, family members, and trained counselors are there to take care of you until you have the strength to take care of yourself.

Money Matters

Many spouses have no idea what financial resources they now have. Social Security might be cut in half. A pension might cease. The double income could now be just the survivor's paycheck. What seemed like a sound plan when both spouses shared one common set of resources has now changed.

Each circumstance is different. There are some who are thrown into such economic crises that action must immediately be taken. A mortgage that is unmanageable, huge medical bills, funeral expenses, and reduced income make it an immediate crisis. These simply do not have the luxury of time. Action must be taken at once. A trusted family member, friend, or counselor can help match resources with needs.

It is best, if possible, to avoid life-changing decisions in the first year following a loved one's death. That does not mean that after 365 days, you will suddenly have the wisdom to know how to reshape your life. It simply means that it's a good idea to make haste slowly. Take some time to decide what really matters in life. Decide who the "new you" is and what that "new you" wants out of life. Remember, like it or not, you are not at your finest as a decision-maker in the immediate aftermath of a loved one's passing.

Chapter 13

Grieving Like a Man

—∰◎

IT IS WHOLLY wrong and totally unfair to categorize any group of people. There are always exceptions no matter what group is under consideration. Yet culture, religion, gender, socio or economic strata, or level of education do offer some stark differences and some generalities worth our comment.

Men often consider themselves as problem solvers. They tend to like to have solutions, answers, and norms in their world of challenges. It is not a stretch to say most men like to be in control. However, the matter of mortality is out of mortal control. Thus men often find themselves tossed into an arena of disarray in which they must admit their powerlessness. For many males, admitting this powerlessness is the first step in overcoming their grief. In a way, it is attaining victory through defeat. This is often neither familiar nor particularly welcome territory for men.

> *There is no wrong way to grieve as long as there is no intent to do harm to oneself, another, or the property of another*

Many young boys are either tutored directly, or are led to perceive indirectly by silent cultural messages, that real men don't cry. Our parents, teachers, and coaches admonish young boys to be nothing other than brave, resolute, and above all, fearless. They are told to not be a baby, to suck it up, or to act like a man.

A fullback on an eighth-grade football team is creamed by a linebacker. The unsympathetic coach gruffly says, "Walk it off, son, walk it off." The clear message is: Real men show no emotion in the face of pain and one's manhood is best displayed with dry eyes. That eighth-grade fullback just learned the lesson that somehow one's masculinity is linked to denying one's inner feelings. Instead of tenderness, boys are taught toughness. Our young men are taught that society values rugged Rambo guys over wimpy males.

When an indelible sorrow seeps into our lives, our boys and men are often ill-prepared to express their true feelings. When bereaved, many men find a huge conflict between their rigidly controlled tears and society's expectation of stoic resolve. Falsely, we pretend the males of our species are not to cry. Yet the great mismatch of the expectation for men never to cry is the reality that our tears betray us.

Deep within our being human are our shared emotions that transcend gender, religion, and culture. We laugh, we love, we labor, and we weep. To deny any or all of these commonalities is to deny a huge chunk of our personhood.

The stark difference between how men and women grieve became clear to me as I watched my parents grieve the death of my brother, Bruce. Bruce was a gifted thirty-six-year-old physician who was at the front end of what promised to be a brilliant career in health care. He was killed in an auto accident on an icy road on his way to church one Sunday morning. His untimely death was an unspeakable loss to both his family and the community he served.

My mother turned their home into a shrine dedicated to her deceased son. His picture hung in every room of their house. It was a like a museum that chronicled every stage of Bruce's young life from infant to physician. Few conversations took place that did not begin with his name.

Though my father was just as deeply wounded by the death of his son, he rarely spoke of the accident. He seldom even mentioned Bruce's name. It was not that he did not carry an enormous load of pain, nor did his silence in any way indicate the absence of his love for his deceased son. My mother was consumed in celebrating her son. My father stoically and silently carried his burden. Watching my parents' grief journey was an epiphany in my understanding of the difference between men and women in how they approach grief.

Having worked with hundreds of bereaved persons, I have encountered dozens of men conflicted between societal expectations and their own profound sorrow. Additionally, many wives, mothers, and sisters of these stoic men feel abandoned by the men in their lives as they proceed through grief.

Tragically, many women are critical of the manner in which their spouses express their grief. One basic truth about grief is there is no wrong way to grieve as long as there is no intent to do harm to oneself, another, or the property of another. The searing hurt that accompanies the loss of a loved one is not gender-specific. Grief is grief, regardless of whose heart is broken.

Chapter 14

Dealing with "Firsts"

~~⚙️~~

"FIRSTS" CAN BE challenging. The first birthday, the first anniversary, or the first of any special event after the passing of a loved one often brings a sense of anxiety. The first family holiday gathering with an empty place at the table is a reminder of that loss. If allowed to go unaddressed, "Firsts" can be a stumbling block on the road to healing.

You can be assured that this is a far from an uncommon concern. It is both normal and probable that your "Firsts" will cause you some degree of apprehension. The good news is that in nearly every incidence, the expectation is worse than the reality. Nearly everyone comments on how they worried about an upcoming "First," but it turned out to be quite manageable.

Here are a few suggestions that can be helpful in not only getting through your "Firsts," but also for how you might consider building new traditions. Remember, it is fully acceptable to embrace the joy of Christmas, an anniversary, a birthday, or any other

Joy does not taint the memory of your loved one or in any way diminish your love for that person.

celebration life brings. Joy does not taint the memory of your loved one or in any way diminish your love for that person.

Plan Ahead

Special dates will surely vary among families, but you are well aware of anniversaries, birthdays, and other special events. These will not come as a surprise. So plan ahead. Think about how you can make that day a special tribute to your loved one rather than a day of dread. Try to see beyond the emptiness of the day and recall the fond memories you shared in the past. Make a list if necessary.

John's favorite food was beef stew and corn bread. After his death as a young adult, his mother and father traditionally prepared his favorite meal on his birthday as a tribute to their son's zest for life. It was a planned new tradition that celebrated their son's love of life.

Be Open to Change

Suppose that for nearly all of your adult life you prepared a huge Thanksgiving dinner, baked twelve dozen cookies, or had the house full of family and friends. It was a longstanding tradition. Grief takes energy and perhaps you just don't feel up to all that work. Give yourself permission to change the tradition. You might delegate some of the work to others. Remember, they have said time and time again, "If I can help in any way . . ." Now might be the time to make that offer come to life. In the first year, you can give yourself permission to make a break with the past. Try something new, but don't feel like this new experiment is necessarily the new tradition. There is nothing wrong with making a change and there is nothing that says you have to do that next year. Think of this change as one holiday at a time. If it feels right, keep the new tradition alive.

Make a Break from the Past

This might be a good time for you to make a complete break with the past traditions. Volunteer as a helper at the local food pantry, a homeless shelter, or your church. Shop for a gift for some child who has a parent in the county jail. Sharing oneself is a great tonic for strengthening one's sense of hope and healing.

Pamper Yourself

Why not give yourself a visit to a spa? Take in a movie you have been promising yourself to see. Enjoy your favorite holiday food. Think about taking a mini vacation. Instead of your throwing the party, visit your extended family's party: Be a guest rather than a host.

Accept at Least One Invitation

It may not be easy, and you may not have your heart in it, but it is important to be among people. Isolation at a time that has been traditionally a time of gathering only compounds the sense of loneliness. Avoid feeling obligated to accept every invitation.

A widowed woman with a year's worth of experiencing "Firsts" shared with a bereavement support group that she always had a plan of escape. She never allowed herself to get trapped in any uncomfortable situation. She went willingly to gatherings but was always armed with a backup plan.

Take Care of Yourself

Get enough sleep and eat wisely. Holiday gatherings often include alcohol. Alcohol is a natural depressant and overindulgence surely will add to your already strained state of mind. You are vulnerable to sickness simply because grief takes a huge amount of energy. Author and Spiritual Care Manager Vince Corso says, "A body in grief requires a lot more attention." Be sure you are taking any needed prescriptions, getting enough exercise and rest, and getting proper nutrition.

Love Lives On

We keep our loved ones alive and our relationship with them in good repair by the way we live our lives. The manner in which we hold our memories precious, continue to live out their values in our daily journey, and embrace the love we share with them is how hope takes root and love continues to thrive.

Most of All, Don't Fret

Having worked with hundreds of persons who are going through their "Firsts," I can assure you that the expectation is far worse than the reality. The anxiety, the dread, and the worry are usually a mismatch with the event. Nearly everyone says after his or her "first," "I am surprised. It was better than I expected."

Chapter 15

Living with a New Normal: Coping vs. Conquering

⤛⧚⊙

Coping

COPING WITH ANY major disturbance in life is a form of crisis management. Coping tends to take on the form of meeting life's daily challenges. It may, or may not, have a definite strategy that will produce a positive outcome. Speaking on the futility of rescuing a financially doomed business, a banker once used the analogy of a partially deflated Mickey Mouse balloon. There are three appendages: a face and two large ears. Squeezing one ear filled the face and the opposite ear. However, it came at the expense of deflating the squeezed ear. There was no possible way to fill all three areas of poor Mickey's head without sacrificing at least one of the other two. Some coping measures are no better than the banker's glum illustration.

There are times in the bereaved individual's journey when a respite is far more reasonable than a long-term solution. It is like an addict trying to become clean and sober. The ultimate goal is a lifetime of sobriety, but it might come down to staying sober for one hour at a time. Stack up the hours, and one day the addict's life is wholly different from the past.

Denial is a common coping strategy. Some sneer at denial, but it has its temporary usefulness. Escapism, as long as it is not harmful to another or self-destructive, can purchase a much needed respite from the weariness of grief. Immersing oneself in being constantly busy offers a mental and emotional vacation from grief. These and other actions are coping skills. They tend to help for a time. They can be lifesavers in the midst of grief's downward spiral. They are stepping-off points for the bereaved to momentarily catch their breath. Do not allow anyone to criticize your coping when life presses in on you. Coping, if only of fleeting benefit, is a basic human survival strategy.

Conquering

The long-term hope is to conquer grief. We have already covered many of the basic skills that lead to conquering that which has permeated your very being. There will be more ideas yet to come. It might be helpful to have some mental picture of what recovery will look like. It will not likely be constant ecstatic happiness. You have lost a part of yourself. There will always remain the scars of that wound.

Yes, you will heal. Yes, you will rediscover a new zest for living. Yes, you have every reason to believe a new horizon of restoration awaits you. Your searing emotional sorrow will one day become a faded memory as you step out into a life of renewal of purpose and restoration of spiritual calm.

The great hope is to use coping when needed as you work toward conquering the unmanageability of grief. Put another way: Your long-term goal is to learn the skills of how to live alongside your grief. The movement from coping to conquering is like many of life's journeys: It is not the shortest distance between two points; rather it comes by fits and halts. You will likely make progress toward conquering and then, much to your surprise (or to your great disappointment), find you are obliged to cope once more. Think of the process like training for the Olympics. You will have good days that are punctuated by average days. Press on. You are on a journey, not a brief stroll. Press on with the certain knowing that this, too, shall pass.

Journaling

Centuries ago, a philosopher said, "A subject is never fully known until it has been written upon."

There is much truth in that ancient statement. Most psychologists would point out that writing uses a different part of the brain than does speaking. There is a mysterious flow from mind to pen that brings the writer into deeper thought. What we might be cautious about uttering verbally, can be expressed in the quiet scratching of pen on paper. Putting words on paper demands a higher degree of organization. It can be reread, reconsidered, and then rewritten. A spoken word is gone in an instant, but the written word endures forever.

I once took a course in journalism. A professor insisted that an essay was never complete in its finest form. She demanded that each word be carefully considered and the entire work be repeatedly edited. Of course, following that logic to its end would be absurdity. If that were always the procedure, there would never be a published work, but rather all the books in the ancient Library of Alexandra would still be works in progress. The instructor was encouraging the students to reconsider, reflect, and constantly refine their thoughts.

Not everyone has a passion for writing. However, for those who do undertake journal-keeping, the process can yield huge benefits. This is especially true for the bereaved in making daily entries into a journal or a diary. At first, the assignment might seem daunting. You might feel your thoughts are too private to express in a permanent medium.

You might feel you are already too emotionally taxed to write with clarity. It may be a begrudging chore for you in the beginning. It may feel like an exercise in futility at first. However, if you press on in your recording of the events and the feelings of each day in a journal, you will soon find it far less intimidating with practice.

Your journal entries are your private and personal thoughts. They are for your eyes only. The long-term focus of your work is not intended for a future generation's reading pleasure. No counselor will ever grade your work. Spelling, grammar, and syntax are not a consideration. Feel free to use an X-rated word or two if you feel so compelled. Do not worry about complete sentences or even ponder the use of a colon or a semicolon. Just pour out your feelings on paper.

Some years ago, at a Bereavement Support Group, each participant was given a blank journal and encouraged to start recording their daily thoughts. Carol was a member of that group. She quite emphatically said she had no plans to write in her journal. She announced that she had nothing to say and she had no appetite to record even one word. As the group gathered for its weekly meeting about four weeks later, a somewhat chagrined Carol asked if she could have a second blank journal. She told the group she had awakened at 2:00 A.M. one morning and felt compelled to begin writing. By dawn, she had filled every page of that blank book.

Journaling can lead to healing by emptying one's deepest hurts onto paper. It is like lancing an infected wound and allowing the toxic poison to escape. There is a freedom in the act of dumping the unsaid and even the unspeakable. Journaling offers the medium for scouring the darkest recesses of our sorrow and then ridding the soul of that which we did not know even existed.

Another hidden benefit journaling offers is a progress spreadsheet. The writer can review past days, weeks, and months and see progress in their grief journey. Having not recorded the feelings of the past allows them to slip away to a forgotten place. To reread your honest assessment of a past time, and then to compare it to the present, offers a yardstick to measure growth.

It might be your choice to destroy your journal so that your most private and intimate thoughts are never known to another. Feel free to do so. You are writing to no one in particular. Think of the practice of journaling as regurgitating what is most upsetting to you. It is a safe and wholly acceptable place for you to spill your anger, hurt, rage, and resentment. If any of these are held within, they can ferment and become toxic to your wellness. If allowed to be placed in a dark corner of your soul to be forgotten, these will only delay your healing progress. These negative feelings will become a shackle on your being that holds you captive and enslaves your spirit. These are best put on paper and then tossed into a furnace.

Daily journaling need not be a dreaded task, nor does it demand extensive effort. A simple entry might be: "Today was a hard one, but I got through it. I hope tomorrow is better." The assignment is not to write the great American novel of your time, but rather simply to consider: This is how I got through today . . .

Distractions

Common to the grief journey is a shortened attention span. Many have mentioned how difficult it is to read and comprehend. By the time you reach the last sentence in the paragraph, the author's entire message is forgotten. Even if you have been a lifelong, avid reader, staying

> *Common to the grief journey is a shortened attention span.*

focused can be nearly impossible. Listening to books on tape seldom proves to help with comprehension. The problem is distraction for the bereaved. At times for the bereaved, reading or balancing a checkbook is like looking at a beautiful sunset through a cloudy glass.

The same distraction robs the bereaved of those hobbies that used to bring joy and bliss to life. A lifelong woodworker loses interest in the craftsman skills that used to be second nature. A crossword puzzle whiz might have trouble telling down from across. The talented photographer might not see anything of wonder to capture on film. Whatever was once a delight is now a confusion.

Be patient with yourself. In time, the lethargy of interest will ebb. The funk of distraction will eventually give way to renewed interest. New zest will once again grace your life. Patience matters in these times of distraction.

Make Haste Slowly

Don was an avid fisherman, camper, and outdoorsman. His wife of fifty-three years died suddenly and unexpectedly. Don was caught in the grip of bewildering listlessness. Spring came, and for the first time in his adult life, he did not purchase a fishing license. He sold his boat, camping gear, and custom-built camper. He had lost interest in all that once had been such an important part of his former life. Slowly at first, but in time, Don rediscovered a new passion for living. He told me several years later how much he regretted having nearly given away all that had once been so important to him. Don's advice was to make haste slowly.

Counselors universally advise the grieving to avoid making major life changes while stuck in the maelstrom of bereavement. We are not at our finest in decision making. We tend to think it will never get better. We see our lives as what once was and what will never again be. We are impatient with the doldrums of grief. While we are stuck in the mud of sorrow, we can see no possibility of positive change. Don's advice to make haste slowly is a sound plan.

Indulge Yourself

Even if it seems more than your sapped energy can grasp, think of small ways to rediscover your sense of joy. It may well be only a fleeting respite from your sorrow, but even momentary breaks do help. Pampering need not be extravagant. A leisurely warm bath can help. Listening to a favorite song can soothe your tired soul. Painting a birdhouse can distract your loneliness. Take a walk. Deeply breathe in the morning's fresh air. You are worth it.

Some tell of the value of a short junket that is a break from the monotony of the everyday grind. A brief change of scenery might bring a bit of joy. Go to the spa and get a massage. Attend your grandson's Little League baseball game. Host a pretend tea party with your granddaughter. Treat your pet to a trip to the groomer. Use your imagination. Force yourself, even when it would be easier to do nothing. Do whatever it takes to break the dull edge of grief from controlling your every moment.

Take a Critical Look at Your Care of Self

This will not be easy, but take a critical look at the evidence of self-neglect. It might be easier to slop around in slippers and pajamas all day long than to get dressed and get on with the day. Depression and grief are first cousins. The two can become almost inseparable. They tend to feed on each other. Depression is to grief as water and fertilizer are to a newly emerged plant. When confronted by depression, which is almost always a part of grief, we tend to lose interest in self. The telltale markers of this lethargy of the soul can be a sharp change in hygiene. A noticeable change in grooming habits, housekeeping, or dress are indicators of depression. To either ignore, or refuse, health care is another sign of depression. Not keeping routine physician appointments or taking needed prescriptions are other barometers that measure the lack of self-care.

It will not be easy, but it is vital to your recovery to be honest with yourself about your personal self-care. A family member or a close friend might comment on the changes they see. This, too, can cause friction and denial. A friend of mine once said, "I said to myself, 'Self, you cannot go on like this.'" A fearless, honest, and careful inventory of how you are caring for you is never easy. However, it is both a lifesaver and the beginning evidence of healing. To be honest with yourself is proclaiming in the boldest terms that you value both self and life. An honest inventory leads to renewed interest in self-care. This renewal of self-worth will break the shackles of the toughest depression.

PART II

PUTTING FAITH
INTO ACTION

Chapter 16

Focusing on Faith

-ꝏ◎

Twenty-First Century Cultural Shift

IN THE NINETEENTH century in America, the general
assumption was that nearly every citizen was Christian. That
assumption no longer is true. Still, many of our institutions,
cultural expectations, and biases cling to the belief that all
Americans embrace Christianity. Statistical surveys reveal that
Christianity has slipped from its place of faith for the masses.
Moreover, when polled, nearly 20 percent of all Americans under
the age of thirty profess no religious affiliation. This is not to be
understood that one in five young adults are agnostic, nor do
they profess atheism. Many pray daily. Many hold the same faith
beliefs as did their parents, grandparents, and great-grandparents.

This group, who claim no religious affiliation, simply reject
organized religion. There are a variety reasons for young adult
Americans falling away from traditional faith communities.
A comprehensive conversation on this shift in the American
culture at the front end of the twenty-first century goes beyond
the scope of this book. (For further reading on this subject see,

The Rise of the Nones: Understanding and Reaching the Religiously Unaffiliated, by James Emery White.)

We are living in a conflicted time. Suffice it to say, we need to rethink the culture we serve. No longer does the twenty-third Psalm hold the same familiarity with many in our country. No longer can we simply assume everyone knows the meaning of "the patience of Job." No longer can we advise everyone to seek his or her pastor or priest's counsel. If we hope to be relevant, helpful, and compassionate to all who face life's harshest crisis, we must consider both our language and the faith structure that shapes our voice. A litany of tired clichés is not helpful. A list of biblical quotes may fall tragically short of understanding for some. Common sense wrapped in compassion is the deepest need of all who are bereaved. Theirs is a hunger for the most basic and inherent level of our shared humanity. It is best expressed by a compassionate listener who validates often and speaks seldom.

Four Inherent Needs

In the face of the cultural shift away from traditional faith communities, it makes sense to reconsider some basic spiritual beliefs that have served humanity for centuries. There are four inherent spiritual needs of every living soul. Consider the following:

The first inherent need is to have a venue for approaching a Higher Power. That Higher Power is called God, Allah, Creator, Jesus Christ, Holy Other, Father in Heaven, Great Spirit, Buddha, Yahweh, Jehovah, and the list of possibilities goes on and on. There is something deep within every one of us that ponders many abstract questions: From whence did I come? What is my purpose? Where is my destiny? Where is my bliss? Who am I? Why am I here, and what will ultimately become of me? Worship is, in part, the venue to approach your understanding of a Divine Being that is wholly other than self. Every religion attempts to address these questions.

The second inherent spiritual need is to fulfill a need to belong. We belong to a family, a clan, a community, or a nation. We belong to bowling leagues, labor unions, fraternal and maternal clubs, and political organizations. We are Cubs fans or White Sox fans, Republicans, Democrats, or Independents. We are Catholic, Baptist, Methodist, Lutheran, or any one of hundreds of other denominations. A faith community provides a place to belong and meets that inherent need.

The third inherent need is to be cared for. Every individual life will encounter a time and set of circumstances in which there are not sufficient resources to provide for self. You find yourself in a place where the enormity of needs and the storehouse of resources are a mismatch. This is when you need others. That need may be compassionate caring. It could be financial. It could be as basic as housing, food, and clothing. That need could include physical heath, emotional support, or spiritual guidance. Whatever the need might be, central to a faith community is the ability to care for those without adequate resources.

The fourth inherent need is to care for another. We call it altruism. It is simply giving to another with no expectation of anything in return. There is a void within every human heart that is filled in selfless caring. To care for another warms the giver's soul. A faith community offers the opportunity to reach out to others with no expectation of anything in return. In a faith community we can collectively do that which is singularly impossible.

> *There is a void within every human heart that is filled in selfless caring.*

A faith community, or a church, does not hold a monopoly on meeting the four inherent spiritual needs. There are many institutions that offer solutions to these needs. However, no organization, no movement, no institution, and no government agency has had a longer history, or richer diversity, in meeting these needs than our many faith communities.

Given the cultural shift away from organized religion as discussed above, the local church is not seen as the natural option for caring in the midst of crisis. The faith community, as the traditional caring provider, may come to some as an afterthought. Many of the bereaved, who at another time would have turned to their faith community, now must seek support from other providers.

How Can I Be Sure?

Yes, participation in organized religion in twenty-first century America is changing. However, it ought not be understood that faith communities in general, and Christianity in particular, are obsolete. The vast majority of Americans still do hold basic religious values. Their belief system is unaltered by those who embrace the twenty-first century shift away from organized religion. Still, it can be argued that the shift away from religious organizations leaves a void in modern culture. It is a void that traditionally has been fulfilled by these faith communities. We need a new paradigm or a return to the proven paradigm that has served for centuries.

Among those persons of Christian faith, a deep calming confidence is in the belief that a deceased loved one is in heaven. That, coupled with the hope of one day being reunited with that loved one, is at the heart of Christian hope.

As a pastor, I was often asked, "How can I be sure my loved one is okay?"

In many cases, I had the opportunity to be with the dying in their last days. Often, the dying would speak about their faith in ways they never before had articulated. It is far from uncommon for the terminally ill to make a confession of heart alongside their profession of faith. These were intimate talks between clergy and an individual that will forever be held in confidence. These will accompany me to my grave. Yet absolute assurance is both ethically and morally acceptable when a family member asks, "Is my loved one okay?" The answer is a resounding: Yes!

I offer this bit of assurance for those who are lifelong believers, those who are newly converted, and those who choose to reject any and all forms of organized religion. This line of logic has been given many names. The "Four Stages of Life" seems to make good sense.

Consider the Following:

First, no human life is the product of a mere biological coincidence. We are far more than just the result of two random cells out of tens of millions colliding by chance. We are the product of the mind of God. Consider the words recorded in Jeremiah 1:4-5b: "Now the word of the Lord came to me saying, 'Before I formed you in the womb I knew you . . . .'"

Before you were anybody, you were somebody to your Creator. Thus, stage one claims life begins in the mind of God.

The second stage of life common to all is in our mother's womb. It is a comforting, quiet, and quiescent place. It is a safe but temporary home. All our physical needs are met. We thrive there. Perhaps given the choice, most of us would opt for staying in this safe and nurturing environment. However, the day comes when we are born into this world.

It is at birth that our third stage of life begins. Though none of us can recall the events of our birthday, it likely is at first a bit challenging. There are harsh sounds. There are bright lights that are uncomfortable on our eyes that have only known darkness. We are surrounded by giants wearing white masks over their faces. The stainless steel scales we are placed upon to check our birth weight are cold and hard. No doubt our initial perception of this new world is far from positive. Yet we soon grow to love this world. The loving look on our mother's face is reassuring. We learn to cherish sunrises, sunsets, rainbows, puppy dogs, laughter, and a strange even inexplicable, emotion we call love. We embrace this life, this world, and nearly all that is in it (poison ivy, bee stings, the common cold, mosquitoes, war, and a few others being shared exceptions).

Stage three can last for as much as a century. Then the day comes when life's fourth stage comes to our door. We call that stage death. It is common to every life. We all share the same manner of how we enter this life and the same mortal condition as we exit this world.

So given that every human life shares in common these four stages, it is worthwhile to carefully consider the journey. We have been in God's mind, God's care, and within God's creation from the very beginning. We have been cared for, loved, nurtured, delighted in, and never abandoned from even before we were two-celled beings. It could be said that from before the womb to the tomb, we hold in common our membership in God's grand plan. Would it then make sense that we would be abandoned at the grave's edge? Never! The first three stages are at least to some degree knowable. The great mystery of what abides beyond is unknown. Given our history of the wonder of the first three, the unknown fourth ought to hold no fear.

Every pastor or priest has repeatedly dealt with the oft-asked question: How can I be sure? The answer is to consider your past from even before your conception, and then give thought to the wonder yet to come. One can conclude that little has changed; we remain in God's care.

As Paul wrote to the Romans: "If we live, we live to the Lord, and if we die, we die to the Lord; so then, whether we live or whether we die, we are the Lord's" (Romans 14:8).

Chapter 17

Living Contentedly with the Unanswerable

MARTHA WAS A seemingly healthy woman in her mid-seventies when she was diagnosed with stage-4 cancer. Martha died less than a month after that initial diagnosis. Her family was stunned by how much their lives had changed so suddenly.

Martha's daughter called her pastor about four months after her mother's death. She said, "I'm so confused. I know my mother was a woman of faith. I, too, believe she is in heaven. But I really want to know why God wants her in heaven and I want her here. I don't want what God wants."

It happens. There are times when God's plans and our plans are a mismatch. We believe in the simple triangle of prayer:

We call out our hurt to God.

God hears our lament and the heart of God is moved.

God responds.

So we have reason to wonder:

> Why was my prayer not heard?
> Why did God not respond?
> Why now?

What is the meaning of this sorrow?
How could God's plan and my hope be so far apart?

These and perhaps ten thousand more questions might flow from the heart of the bereaved.

Many people of faith attempt to explain this great mystery. Some use clichés that seem to make sense on one level but bring little lasting comfort. Some quote Scripture that brings a twinkle of understanding to a few. The fact is, not even the world's most brilliant theologians can definitively answer these questions. The best we mortals can do is accept the fact that in the divine universe there is a greater plan than we can comprehend. Maybe in some future dimension and in some deeper wisdom than we now possess, we will get a glimmer of understanding. Or as Paul puts it: "Now I know only in part; then I will know fully" (1 Corinthians 13:12).

The bereaved daughter's pondering about the void between God's will and her hope is far from unusual. To lash out at God or take a hiatus from a lifetime of faith in the face of grief is not uncommon. Many apologetically admit they are angry with God. Some stalwart believers hold this rage within and never allow another to hear their words of secret contempt for God's plan. No one could begin to count the number of times it has been said, "Why did God take him or her?"

First, know your unanswerable questions are far from firsts. It is part of the mortal condition. This does not mean you are weak-willed or that your faith has failed you. We tend not to read the fine print on the bottom of the page of life that explains our mortality. We just check, "ACCEPT" and get on with life. Death is a real and an unavoidable part of living. We cling to this life with such tenacity and embrace the wonders of this world with such relish that death seems a cruel verdict. Yet the author of all Creation and our individual lives had this full circle in mind from the very beginning. Surely, there is more than we can here behold.

Second, when you feel angry with God be assured God has heard it all before. Remember, God hears our lament and the heart of God is moved. God gets it! God will not send a bolt of lightning to quell our insolence. God fully understands the close relationship between our sorrow and our rage. It would be a paranoid and puny god who felt compelled to teach us a lesson in our already darkest moment. If you are angry with God, say so. God is perfectly okay with your honesty. God has heard it all before. Also, do you really think you can feel such anger and hide it from an all-knowing God?

> *God is perfectly okay with your honesty. God has heard it all before.*

Be as bold as you must in expressing your rage and as quizzical as you can be in asking life's unanswerable questions. It is the beginning of the road toward healing. An honest and open heart is a hollow place that welcomes new comfort, hope, and healing.

Third, embrace the unanswerable as a positive force. If any one of us could fully understand the enormity of God's mind, we would have reduced God to no more than our human mind. If that were true, we would have no need for God because we now would have the mind of God. The Creator of the universe is bigger than any mortal mind can contain. If the totality of God, and God's grand plan, could possibly be contained in any human mind, our Creator would indeed be a puny and rather insignificant god. Greet the unanswerable with an acceptance that the divine has wisdom far beyond any of us.

Finally, beware of "Fixers" and welcome "Listeners." Your greatest need in healing is a quiet, affirming, compassionate listener. Such an individual is far more valuable than a professional fixer. Pastors, counselors, friends, and family who, in their genuine concern, try to answer the unanswerable are misinformed at best and frauds at worst. Those who listen with compassionate hearts are the wise healers you most need.

The present sorrow that is yours as a bereaved person cannot be soothed with simple answers. Yours is a journey into an unexplored realm. There will be tears shed, lessons learned, understandings that will remain elusive, memories fondly embraced, bitterness soothed, and growth beyond your imagination. It takes time and it takes an honest and open heart to come to a place of acceptance. The greatest goal you can now have is not to know the answers to the unanswerable, but rather to come to a time of acceptance.

Ask the unanswerable if you must and shake your angry fist at God if you like. These are the evidence of honestly expressing your grief. Keep an open heart. Consider setting a new goal. For any among us to know all the answers is not achievable. For the bereaved, the greatest goal is to build the skills that lead to contentedly living alongside your sorrow.

Chapter 18

Bitter or Better

~⚮◯

HE WAS A nineteen-year-old farm boy from Iowa. The frigid blast of near-zero wind stung his cheeks. The snow came horizontal to the frozen ground. This was no prairie blast across a barren Iowa cornfield in the middle of winter. The place was a grim battlefield in Belgium. It was December 1944, as the Battle of the Bulge rained terror from the skies.

A German mortar round landed near the young man's foxhole. He was grievously wounded. Medics scooped up what was left of him and rushed him to a field first aid camp. They patched him up and immediately shipped him to a military hospital. His wounds were extensive. He had lost his left eye and his left arm along with an alarming amount of blood. He would survive, but he had a long road to recovery ahead of him.

Eventually the lad from Iowa was sent to recuperate in a military facility in England. An Army chaplain pulled up a stool beside the boy's bed and asked how he was doing. The soldier shrugged his shoulders and said, "Okay, I guess."

The chaplain sat quietly for a moment, as if he were carefully considering his words. Then he said, "Son, you have two choices. You can get better or you can get bitter, but you cannot do both."

The Iowa farm boy would get better. Years later he would become the director of one of America's largest Christian counseling clinics.

It has been said many ways. Life's challenges are inevitable; how we respond to life's challenges is optional. Crisis can birth a new spirit. Out of gray rock tossed into the smelting furnace comes liquid gold. We, too, have the opportunity to use our darkest moments as the catalyst for a new beginning. It is often a matter of choice. The option to remain a victim is ours. So, too, is the opportunity to find renewal, restoration, and redemption.

> *Life's challenges are inevitable; how we respond to life's challenges is optional.*

You can become bitter. You can blame others. You can wallow in misery. Or a new you can be birthed from life's deepest despair. Bitter or better is a matter of choice.

An anonymous poet put it this way: "I pray not to be bitterly disappointed that roses have thorns, but rather to be supremely grateful that thorns have roses."

It truly is a matter of perspective. The rub for the bereaved is that making the choice may not be as easy as simply deciding to choose better over bitter. The bereaved need encouraging people. They need family, friends, or professionals who listen to them and validate them in their time of grief. Those well-meaning souls who have stock answers to all of life's mysteries and heartbreaks are to be avoided. Politely steer clear of those who have a storehouse of sentences that begin with: "What you need to do . . ." Your greatest need is a compassionate listener rather than a sack of solutions.

You are on a journey that will, in time, lead to recovery. It is essential to believe that hope can, and will, be restored to your current hopeless condition. That belief is far more than mere optimism. That hope is the core of faith in the future. It is not one that demands, nor expects, instant results. It is rather a confidence in a positive restoration of a life of meaning, purpose, and reasonable happiness. It is confidence that your brokenness will be healed.

There is a stark difference between cure and healing. Cure is the absence of all pathogens. To be healed is to come to a spiritual harmony with one's affliction. It is interesting that Jesus healed the sick, the lame, and the leper. He did not cure them. Every one of those whom Jesus healed is now dead, but it can be argued that every one of them still basks in the wonder of that spiritual healing. A cure deals with a physical or mental disease. On the other hand, a healing focuses on the dis-ease of the afflicted. The ill-at-ease, the discomforted, and the dis-eased all long for the lasting wonder of healing rather than the transient relief of cure.

Consider a patient who has a terminal illness: The medical community uses every asset it has to bring about a cure. Many are successful, but there are those conditions that do not respond to the best that modern medicine has to offer. It could be said the patient failed to be cured. However, suppose the patient had a spiritual awakening that led him or her to a time of acceptance. The patient discovered a spiritual harmony that birthed a measure of bliss, comfort, and acceptance into their life. The disease was still thriving within the person, but the dis-ease was no longer a threat. The dis-ease had been put to rest by a spiritual awakening within. Thus healing is eternal and all-encompassing, while cure is only a respite from our mortal condition.

The bereaved seek healing. Healing can, and often does, take time. It is a journey through the ugly desert of grief. There will be stops along the way. There will be times of great progress. There will be questioning and seeking reassurance that you are on the right path toward your horizon of hope. It is not a race, nor is it a competition. No medal will be awarded to the first who reaches the promised land of hope. It is not a sprint to the goal. Rather, healing is more like a 10K race.

This is an uncharted course where a quiet and assuring guide can be of enormous help. Resist any invitations to take a shortcut. Gently turn down those who offer a ride in their shiny dune buggy across this desert of discontent. A focused and deliberate effort to do the hard work of mourning is not easy. However, it does not have to be a solitary trudge. There are those who are there to help. Choose your traveling companions carefully as you focus on the certain goal of rediscovering hope. As tempting as it may seem in choosing bitter over better, leave bitter behind. Bitterness and victimhood can be seductive temptations. Choosing bitter over better is a harmful oasis that atrophies any hope for your healing and recovery.

Chapter 19

On the Power of Prayer

⤚⟨⟩⟆

AT A SUPPORT group gathering, I once heard a young man say, "I'm lost in prayer. I don't know what words to use, or where to even begin."

Seated across the table from that well-dressed young man was an elderly woman. She was poorly dressed. She wore the scars of having lived a tough life. Her hair was unkempt and there were a few missing front teeth. She was not the picture that comes to mind when one considers the mental picture of a wise sage.

The old woman said, "Prayer ought not be a problem. Picking the right words is easy if you remember you are talking to your oldest and dearest friend."

The old woman's words were wonderfully simplistic and absolutely true.

So who is your oldest and dearest friend? Is your friend compassionate and caring, or is your friend one of absolute authority and filled with vengeance?

Your image of God has everything to do with how that conversation will go. If your concept of God is one of wrath who delights in imposing misery upon you for some real or imagined misbehavior, finding hope and healing is going to be elusive.

I have heard many say, "I don't know what I did to deserve this." The fact is, you did nothing to deserve the grief you now bear from the death of a loved one. God does not work like that. It is not God's good pleasure to hand out misery simply to make us love, respect, and obey God's divine will. God is not the author of misery. The heart of God finds no delight in the tears of the bereaved. Rather, God weeps with you. It is this simple: A God concept of a divine being who is filled with anger, rage, and vengeance holds little hope for healing. A God concept of grace, mercy, and compassion offers great hope.

If you understand God as filled with compassion, mercy, and grace it would follow that your restoration of hope and healing is shared by your Creator. How you understand the nature of God is vital to healing. Thus your God concept shapes the conversation you have with God. If you are, as the toothless old woman said, "talking to your oldest and dearest friend," your understanding of that friendship means everything to the words you choose. You need not cower down and regurgitate your shame and shortcomings before the Holy. Rather, if you are hurting, simply say, "God, my heart is broken."

> *If you are hurting, simply say, "God, my heart is broken."*

In an earlier chapter we discussed the three-pronged nature of prayer. They are:

God hears the lament of the people.

The heart of God is moved.

God responds.

How you understand the nature of that listening God shapes and informs the language and the hope you bring to that intimate conversation.

Occasionally someone will say, "I'm worried. Oh, sure, I've prayed, but I'm still worried."

One cannot simultaneously worry and pray. The two are incongruent. Prayer and worry are like water and oil; they simply do not mix. If you choose to pray, you have abandoned your will and your crisis to God. If you choose to worry, you are withholding your faith in prayer. A worrisome prayer is a conditional prayer filled with reservation. To put it another way, if you choose to worry, then do not bother God with your prayers.

Totally abandoning our worry to God's will is the hinge pin of faith. To be sure, that is a brave act. It might not come as your first option. Prayer with a tiny bit of reservation is reasonable in the beginning. Growth in faith is the ability to turn your greatest burdens over to God and to then live with a sense of confidence that in the overall scheme of things, all will be well.

Chapter 20

Honesty

~∰⊙

I HAVE OFTEN been asked how a bereavement support groups works. The best answer I can find is: Just fine. Actually, I do not know the totality of ingredients that make a support group so successful. Perhaps there is no single answer. However, I have come to believe that a safe and nonjudgmental place to be honest with one's grief is at least part of the winning formula.

> *To be honest with one's grief is at least part of the winning formula.*

My best teachers, in my role as a grief counselor, were not found in some university or seminary classroom. My best teachers offer no plaques to hang on an office wall. Those who have taught me most about grief are those with whom I have been invited to be a fellow traveler in their grief journey. It is their honest and fearless sharing that has been my instructor. Their stories, stripped of any beauty, standing unclothed in the sunlight of truth and seen in its rawness, have shaped and informed my understanding of grief.

It was the third week of an eight-week group session. For the first two weeks the woman had either said, "Pass," or had little otherwise to say. This evening she had plenty to say. She said, "How I wish I could be as sad about my husband's death as the rest of you are for your loss. I'm ashamed to say it, but I'm glad he's dead. He was a drunk and a womanizer. He used me for his punching bag for forty years. I wish I could say I'm sorry, but I'm not."

The room grew uncomfortably quiet. Then a man broke the silence. He said, "My wife was a lifelong spender. No matter how much money I made, she spent it all and then some. I have been working at sorting her personal items. What am I going to do with more than three hundred pairs of shoes? I'm old and I'm broke. I resent her spending thousands of dollars on those shoes. They are a visible reminder of her squandering lifestyle."

Those were back-to-back lessons in the depth of anger that is far from uncommon among the grieving. They are also a testimony of the power of trust these two hurting individuals placed in the group. It took guts to be so honest. It took a deep sense of knowing that what is said here, stays here. They had found a safe place to vent their rage.

As mentioned earlier, in 1969, Elizabeth Kubler-Ross published the seminal and pioneering work, *On Death and Dying*. Kubler-Ross identified five often-quoted stages shared by both the dying and the bereaved. They are: denial, anger, bargaining, depression, and acceptance. We have briefly explored denial and depression earlier in this book. For the grieving, bargaining most often is expressed in questioning the reasons for this present hurt. In a later section we will discuss acceptance.

Let us now further consider the unwelcome and uncomfortable stage of anger. A major part of grieving is anger. There are ample targets on which to draw the crosshairs of anger. Sometimes the deceased is the target of that rage. If he had only listened to the doctors. If she had taken her prescriptions. If he had quit smoking. If she had stopped drinking. If he had not been so risky. Had the physicians not been so careless with her care. Had that other woman not been part of the picture. The list goes on. There is no shortage of places to point one's anger. A woman whose husband had died recently said, "Sometimes I'm angry for no reason at all. The rage just rises in my throat and nearly chokes me. I feel like my anger has robbed me of oxygen."

It would be so easy if one could just say, "There, there. Take a timeout from anger." Tragically, it is not that easy. The beginning of dealing with anger is to recognize the futility of rage. Carrying the baggage of resentments or lugging a suitcase filled with rage are burdens too great to bear. Pushing the mud-boat of anger up the hill of reason is exhausting. It takes a lot of energy to travel the road of recovery. One must travel light if progress is to be realized. Take an inventory of your anger. Enjoy it for as short a time as possible, and then dig a hole, put your anger in the hole, and cover it up. When that is done, dig a second hole to bury the shovel and then stomp dirt on it with all your weight.

Simply put: Anger, rage, and resentment are luxuries you cannot afford.

Take that fearless and searching examination to size up your level of anger. If you are honest, you will surely find some. Identify a trusted person or persons with whom to share your angry findings. Then leave it behind. You will have excised the malignancy from your soul. You are then ready to move on.

Suppose your anger and rage are just too much for you to share with another. Does that mean you are doomed to wallow in your anger for the rest of your life? No. There is one who is always willing to listen to the meditations and petitions of your heart. Take your desire to be rid of your anger to God. Sincerely and earnestly petition God to cleanse your soul of this uninvited guest. Acknowledge before God that this burden is too much for you to bear. Ask that it be lifted. Be confident God has heard your petition, the heart of God is moved, and that toxic anger will be soothed. God fully understands how the anchor of anger denies your progress. God wants better for you and is both fully capable and willing to remove this load that impedes progress.

Consider the words of the author of Ecclesiastes: "Do not be quick to anger, for anger lodges in the bosom of fools" (Ecclesiastes 7:9).

Add to that thought what Jesus' brother James wrote: "You must understand this, my beloved: let everyone be quick to listen, slow to speak, slow to anger; for your anger does not produce God's righteousness" (James 1:19-20).

From the above, it would seem that anger makes us unrighteous fools. It is a price far too high to pay. Again, it is an unaffordable luxury.

Sounds easy? No, it is not. Most undertakings that are life-shaping are not easy. It begins with an honest search of your deepest self. The reward is certain progress toward finding hope and restoration. The cost of keeping your anger is too great. To choose to hang on to your anger will bog you down and either will prolong your recovery or keep it at a permanent distance. The ultimate cost of keeping your anger is to become a bitter or cynical person with an atrophied spirit. The ultimate reward is restored hope, healing, and renewal.

Chapter 21

You Are Forever Changed

THE PUREST GOLD is refined in the smelter's furnace. Tempered steel is many times stronger than its sibling, untempered iron. The same is true for every life. Having endured great hardship or having overcome a crisis makes us stronger. It is often said, "That which does not kill us makes us stronger." An exception to that old adage might be a hungry or an angry bear.

No one invites suffering into his or her life just to become a more resolute individual. Who would ever volunteer for grief to come and reside in their life in order to become stronger? It would be as absurd as reclining on a bed of nails with the intent of developing a deeper appreciation for your mattress.

However, having descended into the abyss of grief and knowing the heartbreak of a loved one's death, you will surely emerge with a new appreciation for life. Recognizing how fragile life can be moves one to see the worth of the dawning of every day. This day matters, for it is all we have. Yesterday is an unrepeatable memory and tomorrow is a distant hope. The loss of a loved one intensifies our finding value in the gift of each day. When your grief journey leads you to restored hope, you will be a changed person. Life will take on a new worth. You will have a fresh appreciation for that which used to seem so mundane.

Having passed through the dark valley of grief you will come to a new empathy for others who are on the journey of grief. You will not have to say, "I know just how you feel." It is possible that your compassion for others will shine through without having to utter a word. What was once merely a tragic happening in another's life will now move you to a deeper sense of caring. You will be more sensitive to the burden others must bear. You will refine the gentle skill of wiping another's tears without having to speak a word. A restored you is a monument to the wonder of healing. It will not go unnoticed by those who grieve.

You will have a deeper understanding of yourself. It makes sense. You have seen what once seemed insurmountable sorrow conquered by hope. You likely will discover much about your inner vitality that was hidden in the past. The human spirit is far more resilient than you once thought.

> *The human spirit is far more resilient than you once thought.*

This might sound like an extravagant promise, but the renewed you will have a deeper appreciation for life, a new empathy for others, and an amazing new spiritual strength. You ask: All that came from my loss? Yes, that and the hard work you have done on this unwelcome journey.

At least one other wondrous promise awaits you. You will have a new understanding of God's mercy and grace. When you were once paralyzed with grief and completely powerless to move on, somehow you were sustained. When you were numb with anguish and felt incapable of even the simplest responsibilities, you were somehow protected. When you could not see any reason for optimism, you were somehow willing to press on. When you felt no one understood or cared, you encountered compassion. When you were awash in hopelessness, you somehow discovered a glimmer of hope.

When you consider the journey, you will recognize what you could not do for yourself, somehow it was miraculously done for you. At your lowest moment, when you were stuck in grief's iron grip, you were never alone. There was never a millisecond of your journey in which you were forgotten. Even in your darkest hour, you were never forsaken. Even in your aloneness, you were never completely alone. God never abandoned you.

As the Psalmist said: "Even though I walk through the darkest valley, I fear no evil; for you are with me; your rod and your staff they comfort me" (Psalm 23:4).

So now you have reached the other side of your darkest dark valley. Stop for a moment. Sit down on the cool grass in the shade of a willow tree. Take off your hiking boots. Let your bare feet dangle in the babbling brook. Sit on the valley's edge and drink in the tranquility of your present space. Feel the warm sun upon your face. Pause and reflect on how different your life is now than it was when you were trudging through that dark valley.

As you sit on the edge of that dark valley, you might consider saying, "Thank You, God, for restoring my hope on this journey."

PART III

FURTHER HELP

Local Resources

~※◎

NEARLY EVERY COMMUNITY in America has access to hospice services. Most recognize hospice for their compassionate and skilled care for the dying. However, for families, hospice services do not stop when a loved one dies. Hospice offers bereavement support groups that are unparalleled in both expertise and experience for the grieving. You can reach your local hospice provider to learn more about scheduling the location of upcoming bereavement support groups in your area. In most cases, your loved one need not to have been a recipient of hospice care for you to participate in a hospice support group.

Many churches, individual clergy, and other faith communities offer grief counseling for either an individual or a group setting. Most community mental health agencies can direct the bereaved to counseling. Private counseling services will have on-staff professionals who can be helpful, or they can provide you with a list of referral agencies. Most communities have a public-funded Commission on Aging that will help connect the grieving with local resources. You might consider calling local funeral directors. They almost always offer Aftercare services or subscribe to resource providers that can help the grieving. Your local library is another valuable resource center. It is hard to imagine a community in this nation that offers no grief-support resources.

Internet Resources

THE INTERNET HAS many resources for the bereaved to research that might prove to be helpful. You can find helpful information on the following:

Center for Loss and Life (centerforloss.com)

A website designed specifically for Catholics is Ave Maria Press (avemariapress.com)

An internet clearing house for many helpful resources is Coping With Loss: 115 Helpful Websites on Grief and Bereavement (mastersincounseling.org/loss-grief-bereavement)

Abbey Press Publications offers hundreds of low-cost *Care Notes* that cover many areas of grief and loss (carenotes.com)

For Additional Reading on Grief

DeKlyen, Chuck, and Pat Schwiebert. *Tear Soup: A Recipe for Healing After Loss.* Grief Watch, 2007.

Enebrad, Shirley. *Six Word Lessons on Coping with Grief: 100 Lessons to Help You and Your Loved Ones Deal with Loss.* Bellevue, Washington: Pacelli Publishing, 2013.

James, John, and Russell Friedman, *The Grief Recovery Handbook.* New York: Collins Living, 2009.

Kent, Carol. *A New Kind of Normal: Hope Filled Choices When Life Turns Upside Down.* Nashville: Thomas Nelson, Inc., 2007.

Levine, Stephen. *Unattended Sorrow: Recovering from Loss and Reviving the Heart.* Emmaus, PA: Holtz Brinck Publishers, 2005.

Manning, Doug. *Don't Take my Grief Away: What to do When You Lose a Loved One.* San Francisco: Harper and Row, 1984.

Manning, Doug. *Grief's Second Mile: Beyond the First Year.* Oklahoma City: In-Sight Books, Inc., 2015.

Manning, Doug. *With God on Your Side: Discovering Self-Worth Through Total Faith.* Englewood Cliffs, NJ: Prentice-Hall, 1984.

Martin, John D., and Frank D. Ferris. *I Can't Stop Crying.* Toronto: McClelland and Stewart, 1992.

Wolfelt, Alan. *Healing the Bereaved Child: Grief Gardening, Growth Through Grief, and Other Touchstones for Caregivers.* Fort Collins, CO: Champion Press, 1996.

Wolfelt, Alan. *Healing the Grieving Heart: 100 Practical Ideas for Families, Friends, and Caregivers.* Fort Collins, CO: Champion Press, 1998.

Wolfelt, Alan. *The Journey Through Grief: Reflections on Healing.* Fort Collins, CO: Companion Press, 1997.

Wolfelt, Alan. *Understanding Grief: Helping Yourself Heal.* Muncie, IN: Accelerated Development Inc., 1992.

Jose, Stephanie, *Progressing Through Grief.*

Contact Information

To order additional copies of this book, please visit
www.redemption-press.com.

Also available on Amazon.com and BarnesandNoble.com
Or by calling toll free 1-844-2REDEEM.